Ketsugo Goju-Ryu Karate-Do
Shodai Jay Trombley

Shodai Jay Trombley (1938-2022)

Ketsugo Goju-Ryu Karate-Do
Shodai Jay Trombley

By Robert Oliver

DEDICATION

To Shodai Jay Trombley, the visionary founder of Ketsugo Goju-Ryu with 61 years in the martial arts.

ACKNOWLEDGMENTS

I want to say thank you to my wife Ashley, who let me join her dojo all those years ago, having no idea it would have such a profound influence on our lives; to my children, who grew up with a dojo and accepted karate as part of their everyday life with very little complaints; to the black belts who trained me, particularly Shodai, the students who trained with me, and the students who allowed me to train them. For the making of this book, I want to thank Brad Lucas and Ashley Oliver for some crucial editing. I also want to thank all the former black belts who submitted to me their stories, Roy Kurban, Jim Choate, and, of course, Shodai's wife Karen for being a mom to all Shodai's students over the years, and the one who supported Shodai through it all.

Robert Oliver

FOREWORD

There have been thirty-one people as of this writing who have earned a senior black belt in the Ketsugo Goju-Ryu system: Alyce Strickland, Tom Rieber, Rusty Fralia, Todd Kauffman, Lavada White, Shane Facemyer, David Griffin, Ken Johnson, Bob Loewenstein, Mark Ashraf, Sharon Griffin, Marshall Van Norden, Allen Crowley, Christine Landmon, Andrew Smith, Marvin Madison, Kyle Brown, Russell Dare, Chris Collins, Jared Smith, Ken Taliaferro, Alan Viengluang, Trent Boe, Mike Perry, Brodie Wolgamott, Ashley Oliver, Robert Oliver, George Eastlick, Cliff Knudson, Tim Bryant, and Armando Navarro. This short list of people are among hundreds of people who have trained in the art that Shodai created back in the early 1970's.

Shodai read everything that had to do with martial arts that he could get his hands on but believed in learning and teaching in a dojo. He created kata (forms) that had to be analyzed. He put his counter attacks together as a puzzle, mixing and matching elements of the different katas in ways that he wanted, but that would always require some thought. Sometimes he changed things just to keep the system fluid, ever evolving. His mind was a complicated one when it came to dealing with people, but when it came to karate, he was simple, effective, and razor sharp. He thought about karate all the time. If he sat in his room by himself, he would picture two people in a fight and think about what the offense and defense should be.

Those of us who knew and trained under him are lucky for the experience, and this book is intended to capture some of his thoughts, some of his history, and some of his students' thoughts. We do not have him around anymore and no one will ever replace him, but we have what he left behind: his legacy, his karate. For some these are just memories, but for others it shaped how we live our lives through karate. Our responsibility is to continue it the best we can and pass it on to others so that it never dies.

This is a somewhat unique book that also describes the Koza City Shoreikan Karate Dojo with Seikichi Toguchi in the 1950's through the perspective of a man who trained there consistently for five years. Teaching karate and running a dojo consistently since 1960 is no small feat; neither is breaking off and creating one's own karate style, keeping it strong and intact for sixty-six years, while never wavering on technique or attitude. Shodai trained in karate before the Bruce Lee craze, before the Shaw Brothers movie craze, before *The Karate Kid*, and before the United Fighting Championship (UFC). He saw it all and made changes as he saw fit but kept the tradition alive through it all. There were good times and bad, good feelings and bad, bridges formed, and bridges burned.

When reading books by the masters of karate and others, Shodai broke a lot of rules for an American. This is not too surprising if you ever knew Shodai personally. He did not stay with his original instructor. He promoted himself to 10th Dan in 1984. He altered some of the original Goju-Ryu katas (forms). He created his own material. These are all true statements. He stayed in touch with Seikichi Toguchi after he left Okinawa, but over time he wanted to add material to what he was teaching. This made it impossible to stay in Toguchi's system. Since he created his own system, he had to promote himself in the same way that all Chojun Miyagi's senior students had to do in 1953. He did not start out as a 10th Dan, but once he started promoting his own black belts, there had to be a separation of rank. He did in fact receive a black belt and teaching certificate from Seikichi Toguchi on May 9th, 1960. The system he learned was legitimate and the system he expanded on is his own.

How much did being a Marine influence Shodai and his approach to karate? The Shoreikan Goju-Ryu Karate that he learned in the 1950's was still in the design phase, and therefore what Shodai took with him was a moment in time. The system he created, Ketsugo Goju-Ryu, is a combination of 1950's Shoreikan Goju-Ryu Karate (the foundation), Kobudo (traditional Okinawan weapons) from Hohan Soken, boxing techniques from Jackie Simpson, Jiu Jitsu self-defense moves, Judo throws and take downs, Tae Kwon Do kicks he learned from his friend Roy Kurban, and material he created on his own. He changed things he did not like, added things he wanted, and had a training style all his own. He was his own person, and his karate style reflects its founder. I am proud to have learned it, to teach it, and to promote it.

CONTENTS

1 The Way

Before there was karate, Okinawa had its own native martial art called *Te*. Combining elements of Chinese influence, it began to be known as China Hand, or *To-de*. To begin the story of Shodai and Ketsugo Goju-Ryu, we need to go back to the mid-19th Century in Okinawa, the Ryukyu Islands.

Kanryo Higashionna was born in March 1853 in Naha, the capital city of Okinawa, during the time when Okinawa was still occupied by the Satsuma clan of Japan. Higashionna began martial arts training in 1867 with Seisho Aragaki (1840-1920) of Kume, Okinawa. Three years later, when Aragaki had to go to China on business, he left Higashionna with another martial artist, Kojo Taitei, but Higashionna wanted to go to China as well to learn martial arts at the source. Taitei introduced him to Yoshimura Chomei Udun, who helped him make connections in China. In the city of Fuzhou, he began his training in a school run by Kojo Kaho.

For three years, Higashionna studied Monk Fist Boxing under a man named Wai Xinxian and another man known as Iwah. Three years later, it is said that Higashionna became a live-in student of Xie Zhongxiang (also referred to as Ryū Ryū Ko) learning Whooping Crane Boxing. Xie was not much older than Higashionna and himself a student of Wai Xinxian. Much of this history is documented, but some of it is disputed. To put in concisely, Higashionna was from Okinawa, and he went to China for many years to study martial arts.

Around 1883 Higashionna returned to Okinawa and his family's shipping and firewood business. With business failing, he began teaching what he learned in China. His reputation was well known in Naha at the time, and people flocked to his school, which was the courtyard of his family home. In October 1905, Higashionna began teaching his blend of Monk Fist and Whooping Crane Boxing with the indigenous *Te* at the Naha Commercial High School. Since it was in Naha, people began referring to it as Naha-Te. Some of his students went on to become influential masters, among them Chojun Miyagi, Juhatsu Kiyoda, Seko Higa, Kenwa Mabuni, and Koki Shiroma.

Chojun Miyagi was born in Naha on April 25, 1888. He began his formal martial arts training at age eleven, in the dojo of Ryuko Aragaki. At the age of fourteen, he was introduced to Kanryo Higashionna and was accepted as a student. He trained for thirteen years until Higashionna died in December 1915. Miyagi then traveled to China to locate Master Ryū Ryū Ko, Higashionna's instructor in China. He failed to locate him but did pick up some of the local arts of the Fukien area of China, notably the kata called Rokkishu, which was instrumental in his creation of the Tensho kata. Back in Okinawa, he taught his teacher's Naha-Te, but incorporated his own learnings from China.

In 1927, Jigoro Kano (founder of Judo) visited Okinawa and witnessed a demonstration by Miyagi. He was surprised to learn from Miyagi that karate was not just punching and kicking, but also ground techniques, throwing, choking, and joint locking techniques. In 1930, Miyagi was invited to perform at the All-Japan Martial Arts Demonstration to celebrate Prince Hirohito's crowing, but instead, Miyagi sent his senior student, Jin'an Shinzato, who was asked which school of karate he belonged to. He had no answer and later told Miyagi about the incident. Miyagi agreed that his style needed a name. There is a classic Chinese text called the Bubishi, and in it are the Eight Poems of the Fists. The 3rd precept of the poem reads, "The way of inhaling and exhaling is hardness and softness." *Go* means hard and *Ju* means soft. Since his style was a combination of these ideals, Miyagi named his style Goju-Ryu. In 1933 it was officially registered as such at the Dai Nippon Butoku-kai, the Japanese Martial Arts Association.

In 1934, Miyagi obtained the title of Kyoshi (8th Dan) by the Dai Nippon Butokukai. That same year he accepted an invitation to teach karate in Hawaii, which he did for almost a year, attempting to spread karate worldwide. During the 1930's Miyagi was invited several times to teach karate in Japan at various universities. In 1936, he was one of the participants invited to the historic meeting in Naha at the Showa Kaikan, where the name *To-de* (China Hand) was officially changed to *Kara-te* (Empty Hand). They also discussed unifying karate—the techniques, kata, and how to promote it, particularly in Okinawa. In 1940, Miyagi created the katas Gekisai Dai Ichi and Gekisai Dai Ni, partially to hold the attention of younger students who would grow tired of practicing nothing but Sanchin kata.

During World War II, many Okinawans died, including one of Miyagi's sons, two of his daughters, and his senior student, Jin'an Shinzato. Miyagi was forced to forgo much of his training while his homeland was restructured after the war. In 1946, he was appointed director of the Okinawan Civil Association of Physical Education teaching at the Police Academy and resumed his own training. With the help of his senior students, he opened a backyard dojo known as the Garden Dojo. It was there that people like Genkai Nakaima, Meitoku Yagi, Ei'ichi Miyazato, Seikichi Toguchi, and others trained.

In 1952, the Okinawan Goju-Ryu Shinkokai was an organization formed by Miyagi's senior students, the founding members being Seko Higa, Keiyo Matanbashi, Jinsei Kamiya, and Genkai Nakaima. Miyagi approved of the organization except for a section that Nakaima included about rules for promotional exams. They wanted to wear black belts as were worn in Judo, but Miyagi said he would never give dan ranking to anyone. He said dan ranking had to come from the emperor's family via the Dai Nippon Butokukai. The part about exams was removed from the charter, but the organization was still formed. On October 8, 1953, at the age of sixty-five, Miyagi died, never having named a successor.

Seikichi Toguchi was born on May 20th, 1917, in Naha. He began his training in Goju-Ryu in 1933 with Seko Higa, student of both Miyagi and Higashionna. At that time there was only two Goju-Ryu dojos, Higa's and Miyagi's. Toguchi trained in both. In 1937, Toguchi went to Japan to obtain his electrical engineering license and was later drafted into the Japanese Army, stationed in Indonesia. After the war, he returned to Okinawa and assisted in rebuilding his war-torn homeland. In 1953, after Miyagi died, Miyagi's Goju-Ryu Shinkokai was re-named the Okinawan Karate-do Gojukai. Seko Higa was the president and Toguchi was elected Vice-President.

In 1954, Toguchi founded Shoreikan Goju-Ryu and opened his Dojo in Koza City, Okinawa. It would take time for his Shoreikan system to be completed, but he created many supplementary katas to complement and unify Gekisai Dai Ichi and Gekisai Dai Ni. He also started putting together two-person exercises, Bunkai Kumite and Kiso Kumite, to help illustrate possibilities of the kata moves and explore different counter attacks a student could practice with a partner. Many U.S.

servicemen trained here, among them a young Marine named Harvey "Jay" Trombley.

Who is the True Successor to Chojun Miyagi and Who is Asking?

There are many books that illustrate the history of Goju-Ryu Karate, most centered on Miyagi, but only a few on Higa and Toguchi. They are all informative in their own way, but unfortunately, there will likely always be a discrepancy around which lineage of Goju-Ryu is the "correct" one based on the legitimacy of the founder. Everyone agrees that Miyagi never officially named a successor to Goju-Ryu, but many people claim outright to be Miyagi's successor or indirectly as the only one Miyagi trained the entire Goju-Ryu system to or the most important person in Miyagi's life (so in theory should be looked upon as his successor). Miyagi's senior students at the time of his death were Seko Higa, Meitoku Yagi, Seikichi Toguchi, Ei'ichi Miyazato, and Koshin Iha.

Toguchi said there was not a successor named by Miyagi, that the senior students voted Ei'ichi Miyazato to be the new head of Goju-Ryu. And yet he also indicates that Miyagi imparted secret theories to him at the end of his life, like the concept of *kaisai no genri*, the theory of kata[1]. Alternately, Meitoku Yagi admits that Miyazato was elected by the senior students, but also says it was only a vote intended to last until a permanent successor was chosen. The person ultimately chosen, according to Yagi, was himself since Miyagi's family presented him with Miyagi's gi and obi[2]. There is also a case for Seko Higa, the only person permitted to have his own dojo while Miyagi was still alive, who trained with both Higashionna and Miyagi, and the one who held a Renshi rank with the Dai Nippon Butokukai.

An'ichi Miyagi, the teenager who trained with Miyagi at the end of Miyagi's life makes a case for himself through Morio Higaonna. According to Higaonna, it was An'ichi who was taught the essential teachings of Goju-Ryu and was closest to Miyagi when he died, so An'ichi must be seen as the heir to Chojun Miyagi. Higaonna goes to great lengths to propagate this claim, mentioning An'ichi as the successor to Chojun Miyagi in all his instructional videotapes. He also mentions different students who visited Miyagi before and after the war, completely leaving

1 – Okinawan Goju-Ryu II, Advanced Techniques of Shorei-Kan Karate by Seikichi Toguchi. Ohara Publishing. 2001
2 - Karate Goju Ryu – Meibukan by Lex Opdam. 2007
3 - The History of Karate – Okinawan Goju-Ryu by Morio Higaonna. 1995

out Toguchi, despite photo evidence to the contrary. Higaonna also mentions Higa being effectively removed from Miyagi's dojo since Higa set up a dojo without consulting Miyagi. Finally, Higaonna includes multiple references to Higa's students coming to see Miyagi and performing Sanchin kata but doing the moves incorrectly[3]. I am not sure why An'ichi had such a low opinion of Higa, but the contention is obvious. Maybe it was a way to remove Higa from the conversation, lest anyone claim that Higa was Miyagi's most senior ranked student and by all rights should have been the successor—as opposed to the teenaged An'ichi, who only trained with Miyagi for a few years.

The facts are this: Chojun Miyagi never promoted anyone to black belt, did not publicly name a successor, and he and Seko Higa were the only two karateka at the time to receive acknowledgement and rank from the Dai Nippon Butoku Kai (Greater Japan Martial Virtue Society), the martial arts organization tied to the Japanese government. Ultimately, it is a compliment to Miyagi that so many people claim to have known him best, but only a dead man knows for sure.

My belief is there is likely some truth in all of it, with some interpretations and maybe some exaggeration. What ultimately happened is that several of Miyagi's students started their own organizations with roots in Goju-Ryu Karate. What really matters is training. I agree it is important to study history, and it is interesting to say the least, but there is no reason to fixate or put more importance on it than the dojo where one trains or teaches. Karate is bigger than any one person and there is plenty of room to honor all the founders of the different styles of karate and respect the fact that they all have their own interpretations and reasons for what they train, how, and why. Miyagi's Goju-Ryu is no exception. For Jay Trombley, I am simply happy he decided to start taking karate in 1955 and that he liked it enough to teach it for the rest of his life. When I started taking karate, I chose Shodai's dojo, not his lineage. At that time, I did not know who any of the founders of karate were, nor did I care who may or may not have been the successor to whomever. Over time I learned to appreciate the founders as a matter of honor and respect, particularly those who made karate their life, but it was never my motivation for training.

Why Karate?

The *do* in karate-do means "the way," as in "the way to enlightenment." Anyone who takes karate seriously uses it to find their own version of that enlightenment; their own path so to speak. In general, children who train in karate do so to compete in tournaments and get trophies. Without these things they might get discouraged because there is nothing but new belt rank to tell them that they are "good." Children want reassurance and praise; they oftentimes want to quit once they get more corrections than praise. Children can be forgiven for this lack of vision due to their age. Parents, on the other hand, typically want their kids to learn discipline and how to deal with bullies, but many times parents do not have discipline either, so they do not understand what it takes to get it. If their child complains that karate is too hard, the parent pulls them out, not understanding that what makes karate hard is exactly what will give them discipline. And when karate is denigrated as a sport, no different from football or baseball, it is an easy thing to quit and just do something else. The adult student typically wants to get in shape, maybe they have always wanted to learn karate, maybe they took karate as a child and wanted to get back to it. Some adult students want to change their life with karate, but it is rare. For many people, once something gets difficult, excuses are easy to find, and quitting becomes an easy option. This means attracting students who want to learn traditional karate is not any easier than a student getting a black belt. It is difficult, but when a dojo gets a student who is serious about it, tries as hard as he can, and grows from it, it makes it all worthwhile.

The other difficulty for the dojo owner is the balance between paying the bills and teaching quality karate. Online reviews make this even worse. To be buyer-centric, businesses, including martial arts schools, must cater to a volatile, easy to upset public. For many schools it is hard enough to pay the bills without a disgruntled student putting a bad review out there that can destroy it. This is unfortunate because dojos are being conditioned to be easy. The once tough MMA schools are now going through the same thing karate schools have been going through since the 1990's. It is easy to find articles in martial arts magazines that explain exactly how to make as much money as you can while changing the way they teach to keep the attention of young students, who bore far too easily. This summer camp approach is to change the material every five to ten minutes, to praise every move the student makes so that if nothing else their self-esteem is as high as possible. Unfortunately, this teaches students that martial arts will bend to the student's impatience and lack of discipline instead of teaching the student the art. It is great to reinforce a student's accomplishments, but it should mean something. If students get a "high five" every time they walk five steps, there is no incentive to do better or even try. The hollow celebrations become meaningless.

Changes in Karate

Karate training has indeed changed over time, and sometimes for good reasons. But when it moves with the times, so to speak, what does that mean? Is self-defense so different now than it was in say, 1971, or 1951? Not really, but people certainly change. Generally, people imitate what they see others doing. If a person, for example, grew up watching boxing, if encountered with a fight, he is likely to try to box. Today, perhaps the person will try to get their opponent in a grappling hold. It is difficult to say how everything will play out in the future. With laws getting stricter and stricter, it may be wisest to do the least possible if faced with a physical altercation. Still, people like to train their bodies for an altercation that could but may never happen. Changes in martial arts tend to reflect the public and what they want. They want karate to change for them, not the other way around.

Science improves all the time, sometimes educating us on the human body, like concussions potentially leading to Chronic Traumatic Encephalopathy (CTE). The news associates this with American Football, but obviously martial arts students and dojo owners must think about it as well when it comes to sparring. Just like in football, just because a person spars, does not mean he will automatically get a concussion. But perhaps repeated full contact blows to the head is something to think twice about as a casual hobby. Will it make one's training less effective if the student does not get pummeled in the head every week? However, if you take head contact out altogether, is the student going to be afraid of any head contact? Face contact suffers the same challenges. People who work in office buildings might not look too professional with a broken nose or black eye.

The Olympics gave the world a glimpse of present day karate sparring, and the result was a gold medal winner who won because his opponent kicked him too hard. This may be the result of catering to what the public may perceive as dangerous. The next step would be no contact at all. The step after that would be to eliminate sparring altogether. Awareness of injury potential is important, as is protection for students. Unfortunately, without heavy sparring we lose an extremely valuable part of martial arts, but maybe there is room for a reasonable approach.

Point fighting goes back to the 1960's, the so-called "blood and guts" era of sparring without gear. But without protective gear, the sparring was as controlled as people not wanting to damage their hands or feet. Eventually there was protective gear and students could fight with heavier contact. Full contact karate (later called kickboxing) was imitative of boxing, but with kicks. The middle ground may be found in the past with kickboxing. In the 1970's, fighters fought in rounds and used the 10-point scoring system, like in boxing. Some associations already do this. Perhaps it will become more global.

There is still room for martial arts to be effective in the street and an asset to the human spirit fostering a healthy life, but certain aspects of training must be maintained with a foundation of self-defense. If self-defense is removed, it is no longer a martial art. Three elements must be present in a martial arts school: kata (for practicing form), sparring (to get used to trying to strike a moving target while avoiding the same thing), and self-defense (practicing techniques with another person).

Ketsugo Goju-Ryu Karate is a style of karate that changed very little over the years. When Shodai Jay Trombley trained students to fight as hard as they could, he did not think too much about concussions or bleeding, and he certainly did not care if a student quit because they thought it was too hard. Shodai was far ahead of his time in the late 1960's and early 1970's when he added boxing training methods and jiu jitsu self-defense to karate. He was not afraid to make any changes to his system that he thought would make it better, regardless of what anyone said. Above all, he wanted his karate to be tough and his students to be tough. He would not promote anyone to the rank of Black Belt if he did not think that person could take care of themselves physically. He made the brown belt rank particularly difficult in order to weed out students that he thought would fail in his expectations as a black belt. No one in his schools ever got rank just for trying hard and making it to class every day; his students had to be serious about all aspects of karate. Tom Rieber, a brown belt, received his black belt from Shodai after beating Tim Kirby, a black belt, in a full contact fight. That is how much fighting meant to Shodai. But he also knew that people had different strengths and sparring was not going to be every student's greatest strength. And yet even those students had to at least have the attitude that no one could touch them unless they wanted to be touched.

This attitude is what students are really trying to learn when taking martial arts. Students are being shown how to defend themselves and get in shape. Perhaps the student may prove it in the street, but most of the time he will not. Most people take martial arts because they want to conquer their own fear of others. This is ultimately why it does not really matter what style a person trains in. Some people may ridicule Tae Kwon Do because it sometimes caters to children and gives belts out just for paying astronomical dues. For some people, paying the rent very well may be more important than teaching people actual martial arts they can use. But anyone with the right attitude can put into practice what they learn. A good fighter is a good fighter, whether they take Goju-Ryu Karate, Kyokushin Karate, Judo, Jujitsu, Boxing, Wrestling, Tae Kwon Do, Aikido, Muay Thai, or Kung Fu. And it is likely that someone who hates the fighting aspect of martial arts but just goes through the motions will come out the same way he came in.

The question every student should ask is if he is putting everything into his training. Only then can a student evaluate whether he is getting what he paid for. The fact is, whether someone has trained in martial arts or not, most people will never get into a real fist fight in their entire lifetime. It is incredibly easy to stay away from fights if a person is smart enough to keep his mouth from getting him into trouble, he stays away from drunks, and he stays away from people who he knows get into fights all the time. Also, if a person can stay aware, but not look like a threat or an easy victim, that person can also stay out of fights. But some people are still afraid, even knowing that. They want to avoid getting hurt, and who could blame them? But once a person has been hit a few times, even in a controlled environment with instructors who want to help the student, that person may get the confidence he was looking for.

The lifelong benefit of karate is more personal. Once a student is past the point of fearing people, it comes down to applying everything learned to conquer any adversity that comes along, which could be anything from dealing with stress to dealing with bosses and co-workers. Everything builds on something else. Techniques are learned and applied to kata, which is self-defense, and practiced in punching and kicking routines. Heavy bag work helps develop power and stamina, so self-defense becomes easier, not because the student needs to be in perfect physical shape to defend himself, but the pressure of self-defense in the moment can be energy draining. Being in shape helps. Then there is sparring, which helps with the most important lesson of all: to stay calm in the face of danger, emotional control. If students manage this, they can apply this to every aspect of their lives. Stress and anxiety can be controlled, and depression can be dealt with, even if not necessarily conquered. The goal should be to conquer the fear of dealing with it. Control our emotions and we take a big step in controlling our lives.

空手

KETSUGO
GOJU-RYU
結合剛柔流

KGJKA

2 The Marine in Okinawa

Childhood

Harvey Leighton Trombley was born on November 2nd, 1938, in Bellows Falls, Vermont, just six weeks after the Hurricane of 1938, which went through Bellows Falls on September 22nd. Bellows Falls is a village in the town of Rockingham. Trombley was raised in a large, three-story house in Gageville, a small community in North Westminster. He was born to father, Harvey Trombley (1905-1988) and mother, Ruth Elvira Trombley (1907–1994). He was the youngest of three, with an older brother Dalton "Dolly" (1937-2017) and sister Evelyn Ruth Massey. He went by Jay, which was short for Junior, even though he was not officially a Junior.

Jay led a simple life in the Vermont countryside, hunting deer for tourists while his father worked various jobs: lumber mill, textile factory, even an accountant. He was not a religious man, believing as his father did that God was in the trees, the grass, and the sky. He liked the Vermont country life, but he did not have any ambition for school or anything else. He was aimless, just going along. He had some chores, like mowing the giant lawn with a push mower. Sometimes he and his friends would track deer for city people coming out to hunt. When he was ten or twelve years old, he would just pack a bag and be gone for a day or two. Oftentimes during these excursions, he would go to Morse Brook, just beyond Newcomb Farm in Westminster. It was a narrow brook where he could just throw out a line with a worm, get a fish, get a campfire going, and cook it up. He knew how to take care of himself from a young age.

By his own admission, young Jay was something of a troublemaker. Once he hit his brother Dolly over the head with a cement shovel and his mother, in turn, struck him on the head with an iron frying pan. After the football season, people in the neighborhood would purposely flood the high school football field so it would freeze over, and people ice skated on it. Jay beat up another youngster on the iced football field, and subsequently ran away. Soon a State Trooper named Trees, who his friends called "Trooper Trees of the Bush Patrol," came to his house and told his mother he was going to have to go to court on charges and she had to come as well. Eventually he came home, and he and his mother went in front of the judge. The judge was the father of the boy with whom he fought. Judge Bowles said, "did you chip my boy's tooth?" He admitted it, and that was the end. Just another day in rural Vermont.

After the 8th grade Jay did not want to go to high school, so when school started back up in the fall for 9th grade, he just stayed home and never went back. His father noticed this and said to him, "if you're not going to school, you better come with me." He worked several jobs at his father's insistence. At that time, his father ran a lumber mill crew and the first thing Jay had to learn was to cut giant logs with the grown men. He did this off and on, and after he turned sixteen, he went to work with a road crew pouring asphalt. Mr. Trombley sent his son to the foreman and said to Jay, "this is who you work for now." He learned how to use the back of a shovel to guide asphalt that poured from the truck into the ground.

His father wanted him to work so he would stay out of trouble, but he knew trouble followed his son everywhere he went. One night he got his father's brand new 1950 Mercury and took some of his friends to Keene, New Hampshire, which was thirty to thirty-five miles away. They went to a movie and tried to pick up girls, but none were found. Instead, he got into an argument with a guy and off they went into an alley to fight. Jay was struck in the eye hard enough that he was nearly knocked out. But he still had to drive home since his friends did not know how to drive a standard transmission. When he came home, despite the giant black eye forming, his dad looked up from his coin collection and simply said, "is the car okay?"

Like many people his age, once he was old enough, with parental permission, he joined the service. Wanting the toughest branch, he joined the US Marine Corps at the age of seventeen.

Okinawa

Jay Trombley joined the Marines in June of 1955, taking a train to Camp Lejeune, North Carolina, then to Parris Island for boot camp. After boot camp, he went home for two weeks' leave, then he was shipped off to Camp Pendleton, California for thirty days. Among other things to get the Marines back in shape after two weeks off, his Platoon 371 had to climb up a mountain, then run down again, over and over. After Pendleton he was sent to Camp Courtney in Okinawa, where he was assigned mess duty at the officer's club before his recon training would begin. While on mess detail, Trombley asked some local girls who could speak English if they knew of a good judo school. They said judo no, karate, yes. He never really heard of karate, but he had heard of judo. Mainly he wanted to learn how to fight. Soon he was transferred to Camp Hauge in Koza City where he would start recon training with Sergeant Joe White. He became friends with several Marines, notably Joe "Ug" Augustine and Mike Deikin.

Emperor Hirohito of Japan surrendered to the U.S. Forces ten years earlier, in 1945, but World War II was not officially ended until 1952 with the Treaty of San Francisco. After this, Okinawa became a territory of the United States, despite Japan maintaining residual sovereignty. This meant the Okinawans were neither Japanese nor Americans. Since the end of the war, Okinawa served as a strategic location for operations in Korea and Vietnam. Okinawa was practically in ruins after the war. Shuri Castle, having burned down several times before, was once again obliterated, this time by the U.S. military. The United States commandeered local land to build military bases, leaving the Okinawans poor and angry at their plight. This feeling of resentment came to a head in 1959, when an Air Force F-100 fighter plane accidentally crashed into the Miyamori Elementary School in Ishikawa, killing eighteen people. The controversy continues today with decades of recorded sexual assault cases by the U.S. Military on local girls with very little consequences or even acknowledgement by the U.S. Government. In post-World War II Okinawa, prostitution was rampant. It was the easiest way for local families with daughters to make money. Girls as young as nine years old were available at the local bars, and enough soldiers took advantage of the service to make it worthwhile for the poor residents of Okinawa. The soldiers primarily hung out in bars, and if they did not drink, there was not much else to do. Some people took karate.

Tatsuo Shimabuku made a deal with the Marine Corps for his Isshin-Ryu Karate school (dojo), while Seikichi Toguchi also taught Marines and locals in his Shoreikan Goju-Ryu Karate dojo. Of course, Toguchi and his students did not teach in their native Hogen, but in Japanese, which was considered the more refined language of the Okinawans. Toguchi was reluctant to teach the Americans at first but did so once he was asked by a student of Seko Higa.1 Higa, along with Chojun Miyagi, had been Toguchi's karate instructor.

Since teaching Americans, much of the Shoreikan Goju-Ryu style that Toguchi was creating would include teaching methods that would not be necessary if his students were local. The Okinawans did not ask questions; they were raised with a sense of discipline the Americans did not have naturally, even those in the military. American soldiers fresh out of boot camp knew how to take orders, but this was different. Instead of saluting, they had to bow, and do it correctly. They would have to obey people in a foreign country and do what they said if they wanted to learn karate. It was culture shock for people like Jay Trombley, who had never really been out of his hometown, but the military bubble prepared him somewhat for what five years of karate would bring. He started karate like most people. He just wanted to learn how to fight, but soon he began to embrace the differences Okinawa had to offer: the attitude of the locals, the smells, the sights of the fishermen and farmers, and, of course, karate. The heat and humidity were things he had to contend with. He liked the heat, enjoying the contrasting weather from his home in Vermont, and found himself drinking more water than he ever did in his life.

Soon after arriving at Camp Hauge, Trombley's friend Mike Deikin, who often rode a motorcycle around town, one day said, "let's go see a judo school I heard about." He jumped on the back of the bike, and they soon found the place. They observed the students, who were quite good, but people were just getting thrown around, even women. Trombley suggested to Deikin that they try it out. When they approached the instructor, he asked about money, so they pulled out all their cash and the guy went through it and pulled out some MPC's (military money which amounted to $2). They started class and were thrown around by black belts over and over, just like they saw before they started, and no English was spoken. Later Trombley would add these rolls and breakfalls into his own system, but at the time, it was not really what he wanted. Every night he was covered in bruises. One night he was having trouble getting into his bivouac tent, his back sore from the night's class, when Sergeant White noticed and said he would take him, Ug, and Deikin to a karate school which might suit them a little better.

1 – Okinawan Goju-Ryu II, Advanced Techniques of Shorei-Kan Karate by Seikichi Toguchi. Ohara Publishing. 2001

First, he took them to Tatsuo Shimabuku's Isshin-ryu school. They had to take a different bus from Sgt White, since he was black and in 1955, certain places outside the bases were racially segregated. Sgt White would go to a separate bus stop at a black part of town called Four Corners, but eventually they would meet up at the same place. When they got to Shimabuku's, they watched Tatsuo climb a pole, showing off the marvels of being in good karate shape, but overall, Trombley did not care for what he saw as a soft art. Next, he took them to the place where Sgt. White had been training for a while, Seikichi Toguchi's Shoreikan Dojo. They liked what they saw and joined on the 19th of October 1955.

Toguchi's Shoreikan Dojo

The dojo was as big as an average living room, but there was also a small area outside for overflow or bag work. It had no air conditioning and there was no need for a heater. Outside a heavy canvas bag was permanently held up, constantly exposed to the rain, making it hard as a rock. There was also a few makiwara (traditional striking posts) set up outside. People trained nearly twenty-four hours a day at various times. Americans started class at 18:00 (6 PM) and had to leave at 23:00 (11 PM) to get back to the base on time. Occasionally everyone would get off the floor and white belts would come in and clean the floor. The inside was always clean, but the outside had wooden planks with nails coming up. When a nail was caught by someone's feet, that person would get a rock and pound it down. Part of the class included checking the floor for nails. The dressing room was a tiny area off to the side when a student first walked in, where the students hung up their clothes and dog tags. On the other side was Toguchi's office with little more than a desk in it. This is where Toguchi smoked unfiltered Lucky Strikes and where students would put their dues and get their attendance cards stamped. Sometimes photographs were stacked or scattered on the desk where students could buy them for a few cents.

The students were a mix of American military and Okinawan locals. The military had Air Force, Army, and Marines in the dojo, but according to Trombley, the Air Force and Army guys never stuck around very long. Students were not allowed to talk to each other during class, particularly when working out. This was particularly difficult for the boisterous Americans, but they learned quickly.

Off to the side of the workout area of the dojo was an area with purple painted footprints on the ground showing where a student would put his feet, with arrows showing how to slide them, the crescent shaped movement starting in Sanchin dachi and moving forward with the back foot. A new student would follow the footsteps along the floor, turn, then come back until he was told to stop. This was the first thing Trombley was assigned to do, and he walked along the purple feet for five straight hours. The next day he repeated the process while the other guys were being brought over to learn other things. After the third day he said to himself that if he had to do it again, he was going to quit. On the fourth day he took his place at the purple feet. After he got there, Toguchi called him over to the main area, "Hah-ray!" for Harvey, and motioned him to join the rest of the class. Toguchi always called him by his first name, the second word on his dog tags. He was never able to pronounce, "Harvey." Even on his certificates, he wrote "*Harrey* Trombley."

Daruma Taiso

After learning to walk with karate footwork, Trombley learned Daruma Taiso, a yoga based stretching routine created by Toguchi and Chojun Miyagi. A local man named Sakai Ryugo was the high-ranking student who typically held class. The exercises were ten on a side and consisted of stretching the feet, the ankles, deep knee bends and rotations, arm stretches, deep side stretches, hip stretches, back stretches, and knuckle push-ups. It was a workout on its own and took about an hour to complete.

Outside the dojo were logs with cement holding them together, making a wall. Trombley and his friends secretly crammed broom handles in certain spots of the cement to make holes so they could see through the wall and watch what was going on inside the dojo from a distance, then covered the holes up with mud when they finished watching. Sometimes they would watch before class so they could skip Daruma Taiso altogether. Timing it perfectly, they would jog in place behind the wall, then run to the dojo from the logs, making it look like they ran all the way there, apologetic for their tardiness. It was considered bad form to arrive in the middle of a workout. Students were expected to be there at the beginning or the end of exercises. Later they would realize that Toguchi always knew, but never said anything. He knew their schedule and if they had a reason to be late or not. He knew if they were going to be absent a few days and when someone was due to ship back to the states or elsewhere.

Punching Routine

After basic stances and walking, they were taught how to punch with the twist of the hand turned down quickly at the end, the corkscrew punch. The punching routine was designed for twelve people in a line. Each person would take turns giving the count as commands in Japanese, one through ten for each step with a punch. The next guy did the same thing until everyone had a turn counting commands. It started with punches to the head, then the chest, then a down punch in shiko dachi stance (sometimes called the horse stance). By the time they got to shiko dachi their legs burned with pain. Then they learned the chop strike (shuto uchi) going forward, and the hammer fist strike (tettsui uchi). Everything was done in either sanchin dachi (half-moon stance), shiko dachi, and zenkutsu dachi (forward leaning stance). After punches and strikes the students did a kicking routine standing in one place, each kick no more than belly height: front snap kick, then side kick, then ankle kick, knee kick, and back heel kick. Sometimes they spent hours just working on one kick. After the punching and kicking routines, they still had about three hours left. Kata (forms) were usually next, then bag work. When they worked on kata, they did it as a group and practiced in four directions (forward, left side, facing the rear, and right side), then eight directions (like an asterisk), and repeated.

Heavy Bag and Makiwara

When the students worked with the heavy bag, it was for kicking and each person kicked it five times with each leg, then got to the back of the line (same with the makiwara). At first the Marines had a hard time kicking the bag very hard with their soft feet. It would take time to build up their feet. One of the makiwaras was next to the *banjo* (outhouse). Sakai hit the makiwara continuously and with perfect rhythm that never seemed to stop. But the makiwara was optional, and not everyone used it.

One day Deikin and Trombley noticed a slab of cement on the ground during break time. They tried to hit it and break it but could not do it. Soon everyone was trying to hit it. Seiji Urasaki, who could speak a little English, asked Sakai to break the cement, but Sakai said no. Finally, after watching everyone else try to break it, he said (through Seiji) that they were not putting their heart and soul into it. He said they were putting everything into the cement instead of their hand. He advised to make sure their wrist is straight, to put their hip into it, and when they came down with their arm, turn the hand slightly so it comes in at an angle. Still, no one could do it. Sakai finally relented and went to the cement. He brought his arm around in a hammer fist and came down on it three times. On the third time it broke; then he went back to the makiwara like it was nothing. The next day there was a new piece of cement in the same spot, which people could work on in their own time. Trombley wondered at Sakai, "imagine if he hit you in the head with that. You'd be dead for sure."

The only time students could talk to each other was during formal breaks. One day during a break, Deikin and Trombley asked Sergeant White to ask Sakai how to position their hand so they could punch the makiwara. They did not get their answer right away, but eventually he showed him how to punch by standing off to the side and punching it from a chambered stance, twisting the hand at the end of the strike, but only punching with the first two knuckles.

A makiwara is a striking post, made with wood and straw, wrapped in rope. It was not mandatory at Toguchi's dojo, but people could hit it if they wanted to. At first, just like the heavy bag, it was very difficult for the Marines to punch the makiwara, and most people could only do it a few times. Trombley was no exception, but some students were determined to hit it like Sakai. Time went by and some students were outside at the wood stacks by the banjo, talking about punching the wall so they could break their knuckles to toughen them up. Someone got the idea that it was the only way to really toughen them, with calcium growing over newly healed bone. Trombley was the first to volunteer and after he hit the wall his hand immediately swelled up. Naturally no one else did it after seeing what it did to Trombley's hand. Thirty minutes later he could not even make a fist. Sakai saw his hand, talked to Seiji, and told him to tell Trombley not to hit anything with it for three months. When he could make a tight fist, he would need to pick something soft to start back on. It would take patience to come back from it, but he did what he was told. Eventually he could hit the makiwara as hard as he wanted for five minutes at a time. He had to get his mind right, like Sakai said.

Later, when he got back to the states, Trombley did not want his hands to get soft, so he put bags over them when he took a shower. He would also get them wet and pour Morton salt on them, then take his hands out in the sun to make them dry, then hit with them.

Kata

The first kata the students learned was Sanchin. The first time Trombley learned it, Toguchi put him through shime, or check strikes. Strikes are done to check that the muscles are tight, the posture is proper, and the pelvis is tilted up, so the groin area is tucked away. On this first occasion Trombley did not tuck well enough, and he dropped to the ground after Toguchi kicked him between the legs. Even on other katas, a student could do it wrong a couple of times, but on that third time the student would literally get tripped by someone in charge. It was not considered rude; it was just their way of training and getting the student to focus.

But despite the seemingly harsh treatment, neither the senior students nor Toguchi tolerated slights from the local people, either. There was a local student the Americans called Chico because he looked Mexican. He was an intense person who, while doing the punching routine, might stand right in front of someone and punch towards them. Eventually everyone had to deal with Chico, and even the other Okinawans were afraid of him. One day, however, yelling was heard outside, which was very unusual. Everyone stopped to look. Sakai had Chico against the wall. The story went that Chico raised his hand in front of Sakai like he was going to scratch his ear, but Sakai took umbrage and beat Chico and threw him outside. When Sakai came back in, he was not even out of breath; he just turned it off like a switch. Seiji was seen talking to Joe White and it turned out that it was because Chico had been beating up on everybody. Toguchi just smiled when he saw what happened.

During breaks in training, a white belt would be assigned to get water for the class, which was a bucket and a dipper that students drank from. Everyone would line up according to rank, white belts last of course, and they rarely had much other than backwash to drink. One day Trombley was asked to get the miso (water), but instead of bringing it back right away, he stopped and got his own drink, finally being the first one to get a taste of the cool water. But Toguchi knew. After the break was over Toguchi, his cigarette cupped in his hand like a Russian, specifically asked Trombley to do the kata Gekisai Ichi, over and over until he thought he was going to throw up. Toguchi knew about all his students, even if they did not think he did. Sometimes he reacted to it, sometimes not.

What the Okinawans wanted was spirit and strength. On one occasion, Deikin was practicing the kata Gekisai Ichi, and his foot went through the floor. The Okinawans clapped like it was the greatest thing

23

they had ever seen. Toguchi ran over and laughed. He liked the force. Deikin had wanted to impress Seiji because he recently had been chewed him out by him.

When it came to the bunkai, or analysis of the kata, Trombley and his fellow students learned it, but they were not terribly impressed by what they were shown, so he and his friends came up with a lot of their own bunkai, which was not discouraged. The thought, at least for Trombley and his friends, was that what might work on a five-foot-tall Okinawan may not work on a six-foot tall American. As for the katas themselves, Trombley liked all of them except Suparempei. After learning all the other katas, to Trombley it just felt like a collection of moves from other katas. There is a jump kick in Suparempei that many people had a hard time with, particularly Ug. Every time Ug jumped, his other foot would still be on the floor. Trombley said, "even Toguchi had a hard time with that kick." Kicks, even in the katas, were typically groin height or lower.

Toguchi was building his own system during this time, and he was experimenting with complimentary katas (what he called Fukyu katas) in addition to the twelve traditional Goju-Ryu katas. He described them in his books, but most people, including Trombley, did not have the same appreciation for them that Toguchi did. Considering the Shoreikan Goju-Ryu system of Toguchi's was a long way from being formulated in the 1950's, the Fukyu katas were not likely as emphasized as the classical Goju-Ryu kata. Later, Toguchi called them unified katas, something Miyagi wanted to create, but did not before he died. A cursory look at the katas shows that the Fukyu katas are variations of Gekisai Dai Ichi and Gekisai Dai Ni. The Shoreikan Goju-Ryu system would soon include the Fukyu katas in the same vein as the traditional Goju-Ryu katas.

As for conducting class each night, Trombley said, "Toguchi always kept things interesting, running things in cycles." He purposely did the same things on the same nights because he did not want people to miss class. On a given night there may have been fifteen people or so on average during that time (the 1950's). There were a lot of students officially, but most people did not train all the time. Even some of the locals like Masanobu Shinjo did not train every day. When Shinjo was there, he might lead them in kata though, usually once a month. Shinjo used to stand by the Marines so he could pick up English words while they chatted. Anthony Mirakian, noted karate historian, was there for a time too. Trombley recalls him being there about nine months, getting maybe to third white belt rank before he quit and joined Ei'ichi Miyazato's dojo.

On Saturdays, in addition to a normal workout, the dojo worked on self-defense against weapons. On Sunday the dojo worked on self-defense from moves in the kata they learned. Trombley loved this because it got his mind working on self-defense moves all the time.

Marine activities

Sometimes the Marines would have to run barefoot on the beach for their PT (Physical Training) exercises. Unfortunately, the coral would cut their feet which made it difficult to train that night. And if the Americans got hurt, Toguchi always knew. Luckily Sergeant White knew if they had a hard workout the night before, so he would usually let the karate students take it easy during Marine drills.

One day on the way to the bus stop on the way to the dojo, Deikin was not there and soon Trombley saw him coming out of a church. Trombley laughingly asked him if he was praying that they would have a good workout? "No," he asked the priest, "what is God, where is God? Why do you believe just because you're reading it out of the book that there is a god?" He continued, "say I wrote down that I picked up a car and threw it down, dug a hole with my hands and buried the car. 200 years from now someone finds it and thinks someone picked up a car. Is that how you believe in God?" He did not say what the priest said or if he even answered him.

The Marines would give candy to kids while on hikes. Kids would run up and tug on a soldier, say something, then the soldier would get candy from the pack out of the guy in front of him and give it to the kids. Almost fifty years later, one of Shodai's students, Emi, recalled being a little girl in Okinawa during this time and getting candy from the U.S. soldiers.

At 16:30 hours (4:30 PM) the Americans picked up their liberty card and went into town, then to the dojo. Trombley never missed a class unless there was something the Marines made them do overnight. He did not drink alcohol, so he did not go to bars too often. Karate was Trombley's only real focus. Once, on a Sunday night when there was no adult class, Trombley and Ug went to the dojo and watched some kids inside after their class had finished. They were still practicing karate in their free time, pretending to be fighting, but not goofing off fighting, practicing. He marveled that even with Toguchi not there, the students practiced seriously, and with no supervision. Ug wondered out loud what it would look like if they were American kids. The dojo ran the same way whether Toguchi was there or not.

Trombley started weightlifting in the Marines. He saw an article in Stars and Stripes about a guy doing a dumbbell exercise called twenty-ones, which involved doing seven curls from the bottom to the halfway point, then seven curls from the halfway point to the top, then another seven full curls. He liked the idea of getting stronger, no matter what it took. Outside of class, Trombley also worked on throws with Deikin. First, they threw each other on the wrestling mat, but after a while it did not feel enough like karate, so they started throwing each other around on the basketball court, which was tough to get used to at first, but they kept at it until they did. Trombley had a saying back then with Deikin that if he did not like something, the other one would push them into it anyway. This led to getting a tennis net, on which they took turns running and jumping over until finally Deikin dove over it and turned it into a roll. Eventually Trombley did it too and loved it.

Sparring

Sparring was done for an hour at the end of class every night, and everyone took part, even white belts. As for technique, new people would typically just swing wild and get hit back, but eventually the wildness would go away. Sakai taught them how to block and strike at the same time, but it was not easy learning while sparring live. Still, the Americans loved to spar, showing off their bruises walking to the bus stop. A few details about the sparring: there was no protective gear and there was no stopwatch. The matches stopped when the command was given to stop, "yame!" Also, there were no sweeps or takedowns until the student reached the rank of green belt, but students could strike to the face right away. And through it all, there was etiquette, even with sparring. Students were taught to never help someone up if he went to the ground, no matter if the student put him there or not. The first time Trombley helped an Okinawan up, Seiji chewed him out and would not talk to him the rest of the night. It was explained to him that it looked like taunting and the opponent would lose face, be embarrassed. If a student knocked someone down, the student would turn around and kneel in seiza (formal sitting position). The Okinawans were serious about it. He also learned that the student who was knocked down should never lean forward to get up or get up facing the opponent. Trombley found this out the hard way. He went down during a fight and leaned forward to get his balance and before he knew it, he was slapped hard across the face. He did not even know it happened until Ug told him. The point was, if a student was told to do something, he did it. There were no questions.

Shinjo or Seiji might answer a question, but only if the student was a green belt with a white tip or higher rank. Finally, if a student got hurt, he was taught to hide it. Ug had a bruised rib once; he groaned loudly from a well-placed ridge hand, and he went down to one knee. But he quickly got up, not wanting to get slapped as well. Students sometimes learned by getting hurt or seeing someone else get punished.

Other rules about sparring involved kicks. Students were not allowed to kick above the waist, but they could kick at the leg. Naturally they would show students how to kick, but the instructors did not really want students to kick when sparring. Defense against kicks were severe. Once Trombley kicked towards someone's leg and the other guy punched him directly on top of the shin. Students could not use elbow strikes either, which was the only technique forbidden due to the potential for injury. At green belt rank, students could use knees to the stomach, but not the groin. In the heat of battle, it was difficult for the student to control, so of course knees to the groin happened. Students practiced the moves so many times: blocking with the elbow and striking down into the shins with one's knuckles. In real fighting so many body parts can hurt the hand, which is why many of the students worked their knuckles and the side of the hand by striking the makiwara.

A standard rule of etiquette with sparring was control. The student had to show control when fighting a lower rank. The material was always presented as if the student would one day be a teacher. Students learned that every time instructors got hit, they would bow and smile. A lot of the control was exercised with slap blocking. The instructor would touch the low rank lightly to show control.

Sometimes lessons involved patience and waiting for the right moment. One night Trombley bowed to a guy while working with him, but the guy would not bow back. The next time they were supposed to bow to each other, Trombley struck him with all four fingers to the forehead. Later when it was time for sparring, he and the guy were called out to spar with each other and as soon as Trombley went down in his bow, his opponent kicked him in the mouth, knocking out a few of his bottom front teeth. He was dragged to the side of the wall and sat there dazed, flicking the space where his teeth were. They had to stop class so they could find the teeth in case someone stepped on them. They never found any, assuming he must have swallowed them. Of course, he still had to get up on his own and bow out of class. And when he got back to the base, even though his friends had been carrying him by his arms to the bus station, to avoid trouble, he had to enter the base on his own while giving his name and serial number. He barely remembered doing it.

Seko Higa

Seko Higa was born on November 8th, 1898, in Naha, Okinawa. He started training in karate with Kanryo Higashionna in 1912 when he was fourteen years old. Higashionna died three years later, so Higa trained under Higashionna's top student, Chojun Miyagi until Miyagi's death in 1953. In 1931, Higa opened a karate dojo, one of only four of Chojun Miyagi's students to do that while Miyagi was still alive. Then in 1940, Higa received the rank of Renshi from the Dai Nippon Butokukai in Japan, making him the second karate practitioner to receive rank from a sanctioning body oversaw by the Emperor of Japan. The other person of course being Chojun Miyagi.

While in the Shoreikan dojo, Trombley did not recall seeing any other black belts on a regular basis, but a few came to visit. Seiji, Sakai, and even his sergeant were brown belts the whole time he was there. One night Deikin and Trombley were on the floor and the tatami mats were stacked up in the corner. They saw an old man sitting on the tatami mats. The students could not talk to each other while working out, but they went outside for water and while the dipper was at his lips, Trombley said, "who's that old guy? I think he's dead!" The guy was motionless for an hour, and in fact was in the way a little bit. But no one said anything to him. That night at the Sakahaichi Alley bus stop they asked Joe White who the guy was, and he said, "Seko Higa." They did not know who Seko Higa was, so they asked him. He just said, "you'll find out. Tomorrow night we'll see him do something."

The next day, the old man was back and did not move during the supplemental exercise part of class, which took an hour. When the old man moved, Trombley and the others sat down. The old man got off the tatamis and stood on the floor. He pointed to one of the students and told him what to do. It was self-defense. He yelled loudly, stared at the young man, threw him on the floor, arm locked his leg, and slapped his face, then stepped back and yelled again. It was an incredible display, and they did not really know what they were watching, but it went on like that for about half an hour. It seemed to be self-defense from kata. And as skinny as the old man was, he told everyone to bend his arm; students tried and could not move what felt like a lead pipe. For Trombley and his friends, they did not know a lot of the katas, being third white belt rank at the time, but were amazed at what they saw. It would be the only time they saw Seko Higa, who would die in 1966.

A Different Attitude

Sakai would sometimes demonstrate a kata and the Americans were all mesmerized. They could hear the gi slapping his arms and the power was obvious. Of course, the students could not talk to each other; when brown belts were down on one end of the floor, they could not go talk to them or ask them questions. Trombley and his friends would talk to Sgt White after class sometimes, but even he did not always answer them because he wanted them to experience karate the way he did. Sgt White told them about Sanchin kata moving in one direction, facing the instructor, but that Toguchi changed the kata back to the way Chojun Miyagi taught him originally. And as intense as Sanchin could be to practice, Sakai could do the kata like it was nothing; after he did it, he could just drop it and go hit the makiwara.

Karate was everything to the Okinawan students, like a religion. It was not something the Americans could really grasp the way the Okinawans could, and the Americans knew this, although they tried their best. The Okinawans did not care if a student was a Marine, all they wanted to do was teach their students the right way to do karate. Deikin seemed to understand a lot of what the Okinawans talked about, the idea that when you wake up it is a great day to die, living for each day, each moment, but he could not explain it.

Walking to the dojo one night there was a girl outside who Trombley had seen a few times in the bar. She reached in her kimono and gave him an apple, which was expensive, maybe several weeks pay at around 220 yen to a dollar. Trombley bowed and took the apple and took a bite from it. He walked her to the bus stop. Deikin and Costas came up to him afterwards and asked him if he really liked the apple since he made such a big deal about getting it from the girl. He explained to his friends that an apple cost a lot of money to the girl and that meant a lot. He took it that she respected what he was doing (karate). Respect means so much to the Okinawans and this is when he started to understand them better. "Once a person makes an enemy in Okinawa, that person may always be an enemy, and if someone gives someone a rock and asks about it a year later, the person had better still have it," Shodai explained.

Hohan Soken

Hohan Soken was born on May 25th, 1889, in Nishihara Okinawa. He was the grandson of Sokon Matsumura, bodyguard for the Okinawan King Sho Ko, and Shorin-Ryu Karate practitioner. Soken learned Shuri-te Karate from his uncle Nabe Matsumura and traditional weapons (Kobudo) under Komesu Ushi and Tsuken Mantaka. Soken emigrated to Argentina in 1924 and taught karate to Japanese and Okinawans in Buenos Aires. He returned to Okinawa in 1952 and opened a dojo, teaching his own style of karate called Matsumura Orthodox Shorin-ryu karate-do.

When Trombley was a green belt with a white tip, Seiji talked to Sgt. White, who told Trombley that he was going to get a big honor, that Toguchi was going to send him somewhere to learn weapons. He came in the next night and an Okinawan took him quickly down an alley, through rock trails and twigs until he saw a gate in front of a hut. They went through a gate, bowing while going through it. They walked up and his guide said to sit down, so he kneeled in seiza and stayed there until his ankles hurt. Eventually he got up and walked around the side of the house and saw bo staffs all over the place. He picked one off the wall and moved it around, not knowing what to do with it. Soken was giving lessons to someone with a samurai sword. Trombley started to think nothing was going to happen, so he started to leave, but then out of the hut came Hohan Soken. He looked like an old man to the young Marine. Trombley started to put the bo back, but Soken waved him off and told him no, "ie." He held his hands on the bo and positioned the bo for him. Then Soken walked over to the fence and broke off a reed, sliding the leaves off. He motioned for Trombley to strike him with the bo. He did not want to hurt the old man, but he swung the bo, figuring he would knock the guy out and go back to his dojo. Soken just backed up and Trombley missed. He started to get mad as he tried to hit the man with the bo and the old man deftly got out of the way every time, hitting him on the back with the reed. He tried switching the way he held his hands, but nothing worked. Finally, Trombley stopped. He tried to tell Soken that he was not hurting him with that reed, but Soken walked away. Trombley threw the bo down and angrily left.

That night as he walked back to the bus stop, he realized his sweat was stinging. The Okinawans looked at him on the bus because blood was coming through his clothes. When he got back to the barracks someone told him to check out his back. He had welts all over it, and he realized a few things. When he told Sgt White what happened, he told him that he did two things wrong: he stood up without being told to get up and he lost his temper. But the test he passed was that he never dropped the weapon while he was being struck. In Okinawa students had to learn respect before anything else. Luckily, he was allowed to come back.

The next time he went to Soken's place it was different, and he was taught how to work each of the weapons: the bo, sai, nunchaku, kama, and tonfa. He showed Trombley footwork, how to slide up and move his hands at the same time. He learned how to keep his position and strike to the body, into the rib cage, and into the shin, then do the same thing with the other side of his body. He had to learn how to switch up how to hold his hands, then how to walk with the weapons. The meetings with Hohan Soken were once a week and he left when he was told to go, there was no set time.

Trombley never received any rank from Soken, nor did he learn any katas (forms). He just learned how to use the weapons. Later he was sure to include the training of these weapons in his own dojo.

Making Black Belt

Diekin did not make the rank of black belt with Trombley and Ug. One night he went down Sakahaichi Alley instead of going to the dojo and just skipped his test. He went back a month or so later, but it was too late as they were on their way to ship back to the states. Sgt. White would eventually get his black belt too. He was a somewhat irregular student for Toguchi, not always in class. He shipped out before Trombley but came back years later and received his black belt. Toguchi left Okinawa in late 1960, after Trombley received his black belt, but he kept his dojo open in Koza City for years afterwards. Masanobu Shinjo also got a black belt under Toguchi, then left and started his own school. Sometimes getting a black belt meant the person was ready to have his own school and begin teaching. Not everyone was ready at the same time.

The black belt test was not unlike the belt tests Trombley would eventually ask his own students to do. He had to do everything he had learned how to do, including punching and kicking routines. It was a long and hard test and after it was over, Toguchi and the Okinawans did not treat them any different since they were Americans. The Americans knew they were not the best at karate, especially compared to the Okinawans, but they did what they were asked to do, whether it was the punching routine, kicking routines, or katas; they tried their best. If a person stayed long enough to make black belt, after their test they had to stay away for a week or two, then when the student came back, he had to hold (instruct) the entire class, just to prove that he could teach the system. Toguchi would nod after each exercise if the person did it right. They were rewarded for their dedication and when Trombley and his friends made black belt, they could hardly believe they lasted as long as they did.

Trombley trained with Toguchi for five years while stationed at Camp Hauge. He was only supposed to be there four years, but in 1959 he signed on for an extension of duty, "force recon infantry", spending time in both the Philippines as well as Okinawa. This allowed him to continue training with Toguchi, at least long enough to get his black belt. Contrary to popular belief, not everyone who trained under Toguchi received a black belt. Most people only trained for a year or two. He left Toguchi's dojo and Koza City in 1960.

Force Recon and Discharge

While in Okinawa, Trombley was in reconnaissance (recon), which, in layman's terms meant he learned how to go ahead of his platoon and look for something, then come back and report what he had found. This could be anything from the terrain, visible enemy soldiers, etc. In Force Recon (Marine Expeditionary Force), he had to go deep behind enemy lines. Often this meant they had to stay and fight. He went to Vaval Base at Subic Bay in the Philippines, arriving on a flat bottom boat. He and his other new Force Recon Marines went ashore and were told, "now you're Forced Recon, you're going to engage the enemy. Nobody retreats."

Trombley was the smallest of the group, which meant he had to carry the BAR (Browning Automatic Rifle), which was twenty-two pounds without the ammunition. Another soldier carried the ammunition and tripod. Trombley felt like it was very unmilitary; nobody seemed to be in charge. He explained, "Someone said we made it through the first point, then said our next job was to capture people. We went forward, didn't see anybody, then realized we went past the enemy, so we had to come back." In his mind, this was the way he was taught to fight a war. The attraction of being in Force Recon was, as an elite group, they did not have to do a lot of the rudimentary military exercises; they just cleaned their rifles for the most part. This was between the Korean War and the Vietnam War.

Trombley signed on for that extra year, but in 1960, people like Sergeant White and others were getting shipped to Vietnam, so Trombley got out in October of 1960, five months after making Black Belt with

Seikichi Toguchi. After he was discharged, Trombley caught strep throat. Once recovered, he was sent to Camp Lejeune with "Johnny Short Timer" status for 30 days of out-processing. As part of the paperwork in the discharge process, an officer would ask each person what they were going to do on the outside. When it was his turn, Trombley said, "I'm going to get a newspaper, go to the want ads, and find an ad for man wanted that can pick off pedestrians at 500 yards." The officer was not amused.

Don Nagle

During this time, in Jacksonville, North Carolina, walking down the sidewalk near the base, Trombley and Ug saw a karate sign. Feeling strong and ready to fight anyone they could, the duo confidently walked inside. They found Ernie Cates, someone they knew as a big judo champion in Japan, very rare for an American. When they asked who ran the place, Ernie said it was Don Nagle. They knew who he was too, and they were sorry they asked, their vigor quickly diminishing. A few minutes later a skinny guy with a cast on his arm walked out, "Hi guys, I'm Don Nagle." Trombley and Ug read about him in World's Deadliest Marine, a guy who had jumped up and kicked the rim of a basketball hoop. In Shimabuku's school he got his black belt by beating every black belt in the school as a white belt. Nagle said "I'd love to spar with you guys, but as you can see, I have a broken wrist. But I can still hit the makiwara!" Ernie said that every day he hit the makiwara, even with the cast hand. They left, relieved because they knew Don Nagle would have killed them both.

Trombley, back row far left, Sgt White next. Seated, Seikichi Toguchi in the middle, to his left, Sakai Ryugo,
in front of Koza City Shoreikan Dojo, late 1950's.

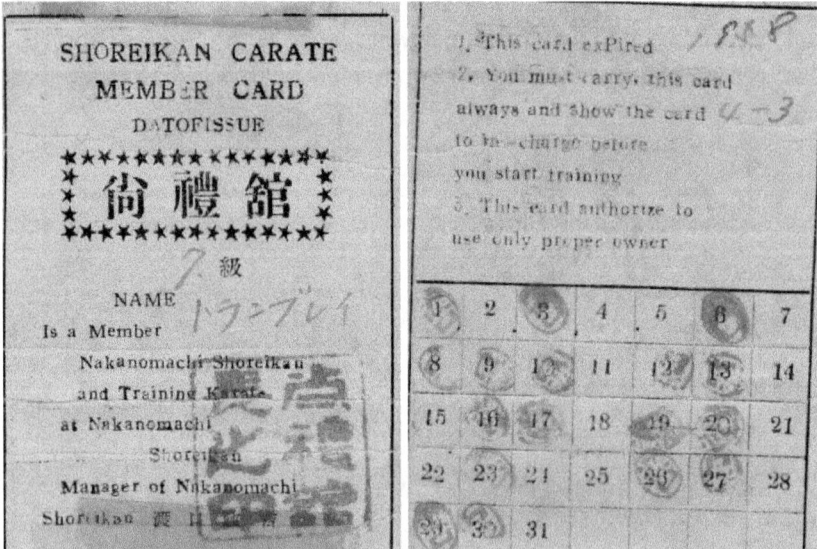

Shoreikan Membership card used every day and stamped for each lesson.

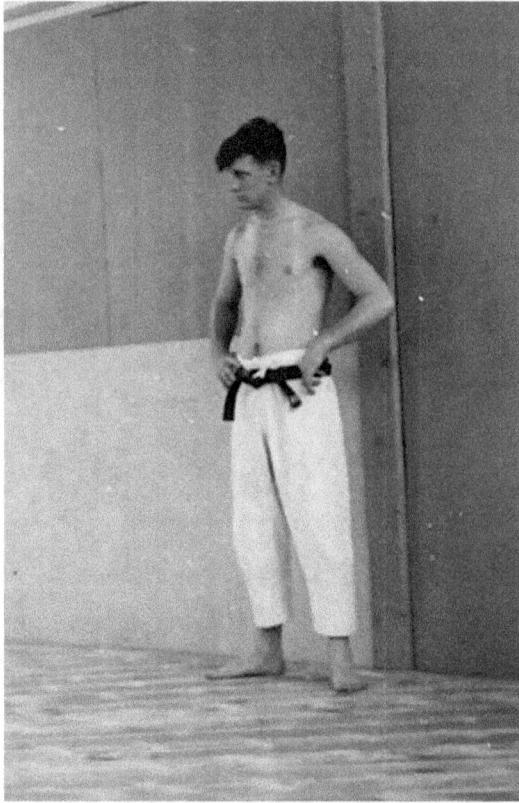

Various pictures of Trombley and friends in Okinawa. Group picture, Trombley second from left.

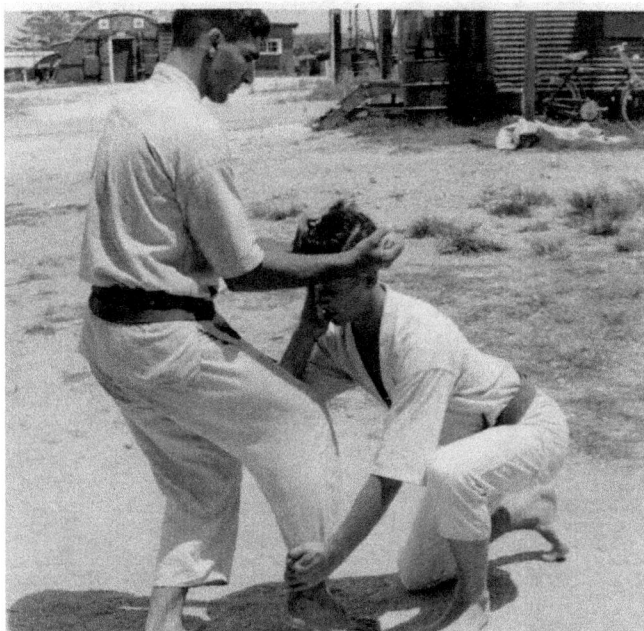

Trombley and other karate students practicing on base

45

Jay Trombley, Marine

Marine photos, 1950's

Deadly Marine Holds Second Highest Degree In Karate Art

A friend's challenge two years ago has produced the deadliest marine at Camp Lejeune. He is Don Nagle, born 20 years ago in Jersey City, N. J., and now holder of the second highest degree in the sport of Karate, Jeudo School, Okinawa, here in the States. The 140-pounder, so adept in the killer sport, must now register with the police department in any city of the United States of which he becomes a resident.

In competition alone, Nagle has gone through 17 matches without suffering a defeat. Coaches have been after him to try out for their team. As an undeveloped track prospect, the 5'9" marine can kick his foot to a height of seven feet from a dead standstill. As a potential boxer, he can break eight brick tiles and a two by four with his knuckles.

He is currently working with the side of his hands (Shuto) attempting to break two by fours employing this method. He has taken six bricks of steel rock and quickly disposed of them with the use of his left hand.

Judo coach Ernie Cates is working with Nagle in preparation of what Camp describes as a "brilliant future" in the sport.

When entering competition, Nagle is attired in armour consisting of head mask, leather protecting his neck and shoulders, foam rubber gloves and armor plate, made either of bamboo or hard leather, protecting his chest. According to the rules of Karate, it is illegal to strike an opponent in any part of the body not protected. Contestants employ the use of their hands, feet and elbows during the match.

Training is conducted on a conditioning basis as in any sport, but the weapon, usually the hand or foot, is deadened through constant battering of the limb against a hard surface, deadening the nerves in...

KARATE EXERT—Don Nagle demonstrates a technique that he has developed kicking his foot seven feet into the air from a stand.

The article Trombley remembered when finally meeting Don Nagle. Note the end of the first paragraph: "The 140-pounder, so adept in the killer sport must now register with the police department in any city of the United States of which he becomes a resident." Fact checking always comes second to a catchy phrase, even in 1958!

FEB 1961

Karate and Marine photos, end of time in the Marines and Okinawa

Mr. Trombley and son Jay

Mrs. Trombley and son Jay

3 Introducing Boxing to Karate

After he was discharged, Trombley went home to Vermont but did not stay long. He went to New York City and attempted to open a dojo in what he did not know was Peter Urban's territory. Peter Urban was the famous Goju-Kai Karate student of Gogen Yamaguchi. He was the first American to teach Goju Karate in America a year earlier than Trombley, 1959. Urban found out about the potential new Goju-Ryu Karate Dojo, then promptly showed up to Trombley's new dojo site and "had a talk with him." Dojos at the time were very territorial and there were no gentleman's agreements when it came to invading another person's space. Trombley was just a kid compared to the seasoned Urban, and he put up no argument. What happened next was a representative from New York City came to Trombley's new dojo and asked him for permits that he did not have, nor did he have the money to get. So instead of competing with Peter Urban, he moved down to Florida where his parents had just moved. Trombley could help at his father's newly purchased gas station and try teaching karate somewhere in Jacksonville Beach.

When he started officially teaching karate in 1961, he had five students. He charged five dollars per month at a place next to Jackson's Mini Mart. Parents would let the kids join, but Trombley would have to pick them up from school, then take them home afterwards. He took out a lot of what he wanted to teach since he was teaching kids. He even tried to associate himself with wrestling, which was big in the 1960's, and he would tell people it was just like that; anything to keep their attention. He signed up a couple more people, then the rent went up. He was working at the gas station for his dad but had to let the school go because of the rent.

In Jacksonville Beach Trombley got a job at Sarasota City Service Oil Station. He got married and over time had three daughters. Meanwhile, Johnny Joca, city councilman, well known former NCAA national boxing champion for the University of Florida, and owner of a local boxing gym, saw Trombley hitting a cement wall that was part of the car wash. "What are you doing?", he said. "I'm toughening up my hands; I do a thing called karate." Joca had seen it advertised in <u>Popular Mechanics</u> and as they talked in the gas station office, Joca mentioned that he had a place where he taught boxing. Joca said he got hit one too many times, so he had to quit boxing, but now trains boxers and asked Trombley if he wanted to drop by. Trombley's shift was over at 3 PM in the afternoon, so afterwards he went to the gym that used to be a church (it even had the steeple on it). "Johnny Joca's Health Club" was written on the side of the building. They went inside his office and talked. Trombley asked him why he gave up boxing and he said there was no money in it, and he got tired of being hurt all the time. A well-built, but thin blind man in his 70's walked in the office and shook hands with Trombley, introducing himself as Jackie Simpson. He wore coke bottle glasses, had no gut, ran the beach every day, and had a golden tan. Joca had met Simpson running on the beach and he told him that one day he was going to open a gymnasium. Simpson said that when he opened one, he wanted a room so he could massage the fighters, time people, whatever was needed.

Joca was a good boxer, which was a big deal in Jacksonville. When he had his grand opening, it was packed. This gave Simpson a lot of business. For boxing he would come out and give his expertise. Some of the guys questioned him to Joca, wondering how a blind man was going to tell them anything. Joca would have them get in the ring with Simpson; nobody could touch him.

Joca asked Trombley if he wanted to teach karate at the club, if he could get a percentage of the teaching dues. He liked the idea and agreed on the spot. He said that he would need to get some students, but Joca said if nothing else, just show me what you do. They went to the floor outside the office and told him about what a kata is, offensive and defensive moves put into a form. He demonstrated a few and Joca really liked it.

Gary Purdee and Irving Hunter were two guys who worked at the City Service Oil Station with Trombley. To Hunter, Trombley said he could make him nine times stronger than he was. To demonstrate he said he was not going to brace himself, but he asked him to hit him in the stomach as hard as he could. He said to hit him three times and after the third punch he would say "Big Black Bug" three times, just to prove he was breathing. He did and he never moved from his stance. He asked how he did it, and Trombley said to come down and take a few lessons with him. Purdy came down as well. They joined and he did not charge them. He needed them to help draw other students in. They came on a regular basis, so eventually he started charging them five dollars per month. He showed them judo material first. Purdee was built like Trombley, but Hunter was bigger, so he used two different ways of training. For trip outs and take downs, he used Hunter, and for throws he used Purdee. The first thing he taught them how to do was roll. Soon he was showing them how to walk, then how to walk backwards. One day Simpson was watching Trombley, or listening rather, while sitting on the edge of the ring.

When Trombley was finished with his class he asked Simpson if he worked hard enough to get a massage. "Yeah, come on back," he said. Trombley noticed his hands were incredibly strong. Simpson said that he massaged the fighters, but he also taught boxing. Trombley mentioned to him that he would love to be able to move like he does. Simpson said, "if you have footwork, you can find somebody, which is what the jab is for." To demonstrate he said to get an arm's length from him and try to hit him. Trombley answered "anywhere?" Simpson said it was boxing so he said not to hit him in the groin, but he could hit him in the body area, the stomach. Trombley did not bring his arm back, just threw a quick punch and sure enough Simpson was not there. He weaved and said that was a weave, explaining about bobbing and weaving. Then he said to hit him in the face, and he bobbed under the punch and then touched Trombley. "How do you do that being blind?" Trombley asked. He said being blind had nothing to do with it, he said it is knowing where your opponent is. He said, "I got something for you to try," and brought him a rope. Simpson asked him if he could jump rope. "Hell no," he said. Simpson demonstrated, jumping perfectly, then running and jumping at the same time, then said "now you do it." Trombley could barely do one, handed him back the rope and said he could not do it. Simpson showed him without using a rope. He said, "every time you jump, your thumb is the rope, whenever your thumb is pointing at the floor, that's when you jump. That's when you start your left-right-left-right, and that's all there is to it." Then he said, "every day you come in here I want you to bring me the timer and we're going to start with five three-minute rounds." Trombley said there was no way he could jump for three minutes. Simpson said, "you build up to it; it's called training."

In time Trombley got to the point where he could do jump for three minutes, so Simpson said, "now we're going to throw tricks in there, the cross roll, then you put it all in one hand, but you're still moving your feet back and forth." Simpson said it will not do any good to stand in one spot like karate guys do. He said, "when you guys fight you stay in one spot. The whole idea of boxing is to move around and try to find an advantage, and when you do that, you should never cross your legs." Simpson frowned on the stutter step too saying, "you should never bring your foot too close to the other one. A boxer will see you do that two or three times, timing you."

The next time Trombley had his two students with him he said, "don't clobber me but I want to try some stuff, we're going to work on different kinds of footwork." He moved around, trying not to cross his legs or stay in one spot. Afterwards he asked Simpson about it, and said he was not doing it properly. Simpson got a pole and said when he tapped the floor, he should move his lead foot to that tap. As soon as he moved his lead foot, he should drag the other one up. "In boxing," he said, "you jab with the step, which puts you in there to hit with the right."

He learned bobbing and weaving using a string line, going side to side, under the string, over and over. Then Simpson would get in the ring with 15-16 ounce gloves and said he was going to come at Trombley, throwing punches. He said not to hit back, just move. Simpson said, "you get in a rhythm three times, then you break that so the guy can't time your rhythm." With Simpson, every time Trombley came in to work there was something new; he added things every day. One day he asked Trombley if he wanted to try boxing, but he said, "no, but everything you've taught me is going to help me."

Trombley would try out bobbing and weaving with his students but without boxing gloves and without face contact until he got the moves down. After bobbing and weaving he learned the speed bag. Joca had a speed bag on a platform that could be raised or lowered. Simpson taught him to use the front of the fist first, then roll to the side, one-two, one-two, switching hands, and never dropping them. He taught him to keep his right hand next to his jaw when punching with the left, and vice versa, hitting the bag until he could not move his arms anymore. He said to make sure there is a little bend in the elbow when punching, not to ever lock it out completely.

He also showed him about slipping punches, that when the other guy punches, he should turn his head at the same time, taking all the power out of it. He said to practice that by having someone try to hit you in the face. The simple philosophy Simpson believed in was not getting hit and then hitting back; he said, "that's boxing." He related everything to boxing, much like karate was to the Okinawans. Trombley watched

Simpson hit the heavy bag and saw how his elbow went up for a hook punch so he could hit with the first two knuckles. They did not teach the hook punch in Okinawa, with the elbow pushing the punch, and he enjoyed the variety.

Besides the physical training, Simpson told him he needed to watch other people fight. Willie Pastrano was the champion of the world at the time, and he would be at Jacksonville Beach with his sparring partner, Ollie Wilson. Simpson said to watch both fighters and watch what they did. He said, "too many people don't watch, people come and just look at their fists, but you need to watch everything." He noticed that Willie never crossed his feet; he would turn and stick. Trombley asked Simpson if that was always the way. "No," Simpson said, "once you know boxing you can do what you want to do because your hands and feet are one. Pastrano was a ghost, nobody could hit him."

Later, Simpson showed him how to stitch someone using Adrenaline 1:1000 during a fight. He had Trombley in the corner with him and he used a sponge over the fighter's cut eye and said watch my hand and wiped it across the brow to seal a cut. Simpson told him about the old days. He said, "the way you trained back then, you went into a bar like John L. Sullivan did and took on every man in the place. The gyms, you went in there to hit the heavy bag a little bit and the speed bag, but when they fought, people fought too hard, so fighters had to get their fight training somewhere else."

Joca asked Trombley one day if he liked wrestling. He did not have much of an opinion about it, but he knew you could watch it on Saturday TV. Joca told him to watch it and see what he thought. It was a local show, there in town and on it was a bad guy, Hiro Matsuda. Joca picked up Trombley the next Saturday and took him down to meet the wrestlers. Gorgeous George was there in the dressing room, and down at the end of the bench was Yasuhiro Kojima (Hiro Matsuda) reading a newspaper. Hiro would not speak English in the ring, but when he saw Joca and Trombley, he turned and said, "oh hello, how are you doing?" Trombley asked him what style he was, and he said, "any style you want, but I grew up with Shotokan." Trombley answered that was a great style and said he was Goju-Ryu. Hiro said that was great as well. Trombley asked him why he was wrestling when he is a black belt in karate. "Money," he said. He said he could not make any money in Japan. Apparently, everyone in Japan ends up getting a black belt, but everyone still needs a job. Later that afternoon the wrestling match took place, and Hiro was there. Trombley was terribly disappointed at how fake it all was.

One day Wendell Reeves, an insurance salesman, came in to get gas and asked Trombley if he was the guy who taught karate at Johnny Joca's. He wanted to spar, saying he took Korean Karate. Trombley said sure, so Reeves asked him to stop by his house. He said he had a big backyard and lights. The floor was only dirt, but it was raked so it was like a proper floor. He was smaller than Trombley, but they fought in the backyard until neither one of them could stand up. Reeves kicked him in the stomach, and he knew right away he needed to build up his stomach, motivating him. Trombley loved it because he had not yet started sparring with his students since they were not ready. His two main students, Purdy and Hunter, had clubbed feet and had a hard time with footwork. He finally asked Reeves to come to Johnny Joca's to spar. Simpson kept telling them to wear gloves, but they refused. Protective gear was unheard at that time for karate students.

Jiu Jitsu Self-Defense

There was a Judo/Jiu Jitsu school near Trombley's dad's service station. Trombley went into it and met the owners, Bill Beach and his wife, both black belts. Trombley said he liked Judo, saw a lot of it in Okinawa. Bill wanted to know about Judo in Okinawa and Trombley said most of it was throws and he had a hard time with it because he was so skinny back then. Bill said no, most of that is just junk. Jiu Jitsu has takeaways, which was much better. Trombley asked him to show him, and he did. He liked it so he kept going, paying Bill five dollars a day to teach him. Every Saturday he went to his school to learn arm grabs, wrist grabs, and all manner of lock and choke. Back at Johnny Joca's he could practice this with his students, using them as *haiawasu* (practice partner who allows the karateka to practice moves on them, but without hurting them). This was something he wanted to put into karate the same way he wanted to implement what he was learning from Simpson.

At this point Trombley had learned the basics of karate, the fundamentals, even advanced techniques after five long years in Okinawa, but he also had a substantial amount of weapons training too. Both at Toguchi's and the Judo school he briefly attended, he learned breakfalls, takedowns, sweeps, and throws. With Jackie Simpson he learned the fundamentals of boxing, different ways to move the body, footwork, and training methods missing from karate. Trombley spent approximately five years with Simpson, almost as long as he was with Toguchi. And with Bill Beach, he discovered self-defense he could use, not just moves from kata. His system was coming together, but it was time to move on from Florida. Things were not going too well with his marriage, and he decided they should move, once again following his parents, this time to Arizona. He still had dreams of being Toguchi's representative in America.

MECHANICAL EXERCISE EQUIPMENT   BOXING

WEIGHT CONTROL   WRESTLING

STEAM BATH   BODY BUILDING

TUMBLING

JOHNNY JOCA'S

Health and Athletic Club

216 SOUTH 11TH AVENUE

JACKSONVILLE BEACH, FLA.

JAY TROMBLER

KARATE INSTRUCTOR   PHONE 249-9512

1960 and 1961, Post Marine Photos

Dec. 30, '63

Dear Harvey,

Let me introduce myself first. My name is Shoichi Yamamoto. I will write you for Mr. Toguchi our karate master.

I have been practicing karate for three years and a half under the tuition of Mr. Toguchi and now am instructing students in karate.

Now I am going to tell you what Mr. Toguchi says:

"I must apologize to you for not sending any letter so far. But as I've received your letter dated Sep. 23 recently because of my move from Sendagaya in Shibuya ward to Maehara CHO in Nakano ward, I did not send you a letter. This is the first time that I've got your letter. I moved here in Maehara cho in Nakano Ku from Sendagaya in this February.

Well, I have five dojos here in Tokyo now, though all of them

66

doesn't have any roof; I mean
we are practicing on the very ground.
We borrow several precincts of shrines.
Because I can't build up a gym
here in Tokyo due to high cost of
estate. However I have about
150 students on altogether in Tokyo,
though the number of registered students
amounts to more than 300; I mean
the number of students who are practicing
actually now is 150. I'm going
to increase the number of dojo more
and more from now on.

I hope your gym will become
my branch dojo formally, because
I want some of my good karate students
visit the United States and diffuse
our Gojuryu karate style.
I never talk I want you to give me
some of your earnings, but simply want
you keep contacting with me and
you and we can make our glorious,
magnificent, time-honored Gojuryu
karate style prosperous.

And concerning to the 8 m.m. film,
I'm willing to send it, if your dojo

become a formal branch dojo of mine.
I need 100 dollars at the least to
take the 8 m.m. film, because I don't
have a 8 m.m. camera to take the film.
Though this expense is a little too much,
if you have a mind you will make your gym
a formal branch dojo of mine and send
me the expense of taking the film. I'll
be willing to give you the 8 m.m. film.
    I want to know the present
state of your dojo. Please let me
know as fully as you can. "

    Like above he says.
Again let me introduce myself. I am
a junior of Hosei university and the
captain of the Gojuryu karate club of
our school. I established the club
in my college this year, though it has
another karate club of Shorin style.
I visited Okinawa during this summer
vacation to watch our main dojo and practice
for ten days
there.

渡口政吉
TOGUCHI SEIKICHI

P. S. You can send a letter, which tells something to Mr. Toguchi, to me. He and his family can't understand English. As I live near by his house, if you send me the letter I'll hand it to him and tell him what you mean. Of course you may send him directly.

I'll note here both my address and his one.

SEIKICHI TOGUCHI   SHOICHI YAMAMOTO

36 MAEHARA CHO   2 YASHIMA CHO

NAKANO KU   NAKANO KU

TOKYO   TOKYO

First of several letters from Shoichi Yamamoto on behalf of Seikichi Toguchi (1963)

Letter transcribed (as is):

Dear Harvey,

Dec 30, 1963

Let me introduce myself first. My name is Shoichi Yamamoto. I will write you for Mr. Toguchi our karate master.

I have been practicing karate for three years and a half under the tuition of Mr. Toguchi and now am instructing students in karate. Now I am going to tell you what Mr. Toguchi says.

"I must apologize to you for not sending any letter so far. But as I've received your letter dated Sept 23 recently because of my move from Sendagaya in Shibuya Ward to Maehara CHO in Nakano Ward, I did not send you a letter. This is the first time that I've got your letter. I moved here in Maehara Cho in Nakano Ku from Sendagaya in this February.

Well, I have five dojos here in Tokyo now, though all of them doesn't have any roof; I mean we are practicing on the very ground. We borrow several precincts of shrines. Because I can't build up a gym here in Tokyo due to high cost of estate. However I have about 150 students altogether in Tokyo, though the number of registered students amounts to more than 300; I mean the number of students who are practicing actually now is 150. I'm going to increase the number of dojo more and more from now on.

I hope your gym will become my branch dojo formally, because I want some of my good karate students can visit the United States and diffuse our Gojuryu karate style.
I never talk I want you to give me some of your earnings, but simply want you keep contacting with me and you and we can make our glorious, magnificent, time-honored Gojuryu karate style prosperous. And concerning to the 8mm film, I'm willing to send it, if your dojo become a formal branch dojo of mine. I need 100 dollars at the least to take the 8mm film, because I do not have a 8mm camera to take the film. Though this expense is a little too much, if you have a mind you will make your gym a formal branch dojo of mine and send me the expense of taking the film. I'll be willing to give you the 8mm film.

I want to know the present state of your dojo. Please let me know as fully as you can."

Like above he says. Again let me introduce myself. I am a junior of Hosei University and the captain of the Gojuryu karate club of our school. I established the club in my college this year, though it has another karate club of Shorin Style. I visited Okinawa for ten days during this summer vacation to watch our main dojo and practice there.

Toguchi Seikichi

P.S. you can send a letter, which tells something to Mr. Toguchi, to me. He and his family can't understand English. As I live near by his house, if you send me the letter I'll hand it and tell him what you mean. Of course you may send him directly.

I'll note here both my address and his one.

Seikichi Toguchi	Shoichi Yamamoto
36 Maehara Cho	2 Yashima Cho
Nakano KU	Nakano KU
Tokyo	Tokyo

1: When Shodai showed me his letters the first time, I just thought it was fantastic that he had letters from Seikichi Toguchi. As I read them now and remember what Shodai said about his relationship with Toguchi post-Okinawa, I can read between the lines. Shodai wanted to be the official representative for Toguchi in America, but Toguchi only wanted him to have a branch dojo. In 1973 the official USA representative was Toshio Tamano in New York. 1977 the representative was no longer Mr. Tamano, but no mention of who it was. In 1984 it was Ichiro Naito in New York. By then I think Shodai had more of less broke contact with the Shoreikan organization. He said that there was a lot he should have done but did not. He said he talked to Toguchi about getting more rank from him, to which Toguchi wanted him to send film of himself doing kata, etc. Shodai really was not in a stable enough position to do that when he was in Jacksonville Beach, Arizona, or even Springtown, Texas. But in my opinion, it all turned out for the best. Shodai was adding so much to the system and by the mid-1970's, I do not think he wanted to take orders from a New York representative anyway.

4

Forming United Goju-Ryu Karate-Do

Soon Trombley was in Tucson, Arizona, working at a truck stop changing truck tires at five dollars a tire. It was hard work, and he did not have a karate school yet. He and his family stayed a year or so, but things were still not working out, so they tried to move to Georgia. Trombley's car broke down in Springtown, Texas and he decided to stay. It was 1970 and he had enough money to buy one hundred acres complete with horses and pigs. He worked at the local gas station, and this is where he befriended the sheriff, Sam Taliaferro. Sam's son would eventually be one of Trombley's black belts, Kenneth Taliaferro.

It was not long before he and his wife divorced. She went back to Jacksonville Beach with the kids while Trombley had to sell the house. He stayed in Springtown, renting a house across the street from the service station where he worked. Sam and another local guy wanted to learn karate, so Trombley started teaching karate out of his house, using the hallways and rooms for workout space. He kept in contact with Seikichi Toguchi, but as time went on it was looking less and less likely that he would be the United States Representative for Shoreikan Goju-Ryu. He was, at that time, not able to keep a dojo going for any length of time and personal problems kept things less than stable. Still, Trombley kept training and teaching.

Toguchi, in addition to creating his unified katas, also created several two-man exercises called Kiso Kumite and Bunkai Kumite. They were designed to help analyze moves from katas and practice different kinds of counter strikes. Trombley began expanding on the Kiso Kumite counter strikes, changing some of the order, and adding his own. He used a lot of judo throws and takedowns for many of the counters, only to change them again when he wanted more karate moves and less judo.

Trombley eventually left Springtown and moved to Fort Worth. He had an apartment with a couple of friends. One of those friends, Mitch, introduced him to a woman named Karen Kitto. Karen had an apartment in South Hulen in Fort Worth and as their relationship progressed, Trombley moved in with her. Within a year they were married, February 17th, 1973. Later they moved into an apartment on Las Vegas Trail in Fort Worth, and yet again into a bigger apartment on Calmont Avenue. It was the Calmont Avenue apartment where Trombley started teaching karate once again. One of his students would later become his second black belt, Tom Reiber. Trombley practiced nunchaku in the living room, knocking the heads from plants, much to Karen's displeasure. He also began putting new katas together, switching positions and figuring out moves in a very small space. He worked out moves in the kata like a jigsaw puzzle. Later, the Jay and Karen moved into a house on Southwest Loop 820 in Fort Worth and opened a proper dojo on McCart and Seminary Drive. Things were suddenly going well. He and Karen even bought a boat, which they took students out to Possum Kingdom Lake on a regular basis. The dojo was narrow and long, about 13' x 78'. He and one of his students, Alyce Strickland put together a two-man exercise for the bo staff in this dojo, which took up nearly the whole floor.

Around this time, Trombley went to martial arts tournaments and drove around locally to visit other dojos, meeting other people in the martial arts world. He was putting new katas together, making changes to the material he already knew, but he was also learning that traditional katas he learned in Okinawa like Sepai and Shisochin would be uncompetitive in tournaments. Tournament katas, especially in the 1970's, were dominated by Tae Kwon Do students and judges, and the katas they did were far more exciting than traditional Okinawan katas. Every dojo went to tournaments back then. Tournaments were where dojos got noticed and built their reputations. There was a ranking system, like boxing, and various organizations promoted these systems in martial arts magazines. The tournaments also featured weapons demonstrations, self-defense, breaking, and of course sparring. The sparring was called "no contact point sparring," which meant the action was stopped after every point was called, and no one wore sparring gear. People still made contact, but it was supposed to be controlled. Trombley did not have a problem with point sparring, but he was not used to groin strikes or head kicks. To keep up with the times, Trombley had to adapt.

Trombley had most of the system down that he would call United Goju-Ryu. It was the 1950's version of Shoreikan Goju-Ryu with some of his own modifications, traditional Okinawan weapons, Jiu Jitsu self-defense, Judo sweeps, boxing techniques, and even a few Tae Kwon Do kicks. It was, and continues to be, a mixed martial art before the term ever came out.

Trombley had a hard time breaking into the tournaments at first. It was almost entirely Tae Kwon Do. Two people that would be instrumental in helping him was Roy Kurban and Jim Choate. He met Kurban on a routine visit to neighborhood dojos. When he met him, they sat and talked for a while, and finally Kurban asked if he wanted to stay and watch a belt test that evening. They were inseparable friends pretty much from that moment on. They did not always have the same methods on how to run a dojo or what tradition meant, but it did not matter. Back then if someone saw Kurban, Trombley would be close by.

Kurban always had a lot of students; he was very successful when it came to running a school, and was well known in the karate scene, introducing Trombley to many famous people, like Chuck Norris. Sometimes it bothered Trombley that he could not get the same number of students as Kurban, but he also knew that they were two very different personality types. Kurban was simply a better businessman than Trombley. Kurban was a friendly teacher who smiled at his students and used his charismatic personality to sign up and keep students. Trombley had the reputation of being too hard on his students, running them off if they did not act the way he wanted them to. Not to say Trombley was wrong; he taught people the way he was taught in Okinawa, and he held people to the same standard he was held to. To him, being a black belt was serious and the business part was always secondary. He could be nice to people, or someone could be a good friend, but his karate was his karate and the integrity of it was never something to be traded for more students.

Trombley did not participate in tournaments the way Kurban did. He brought students, but he did compete once in a Micki Fisher tournament at Love Field Airport in Dallas. Trombley performed Seiunchin kata and uncharacteristically slipped going down in one of the opening moves. He made up some moves to cover his mistake and received second place from the judges. Afterwards Luther Duffy, friend and fellow karate practitioner, asked him about it, "I've never seen that kata before." Trombley joked, "Oh that's a great kata in our system," and Duffy said, "I don't believe you. What was the name of it?" Trombley answered, "the one I started or the one I finished?" Trombley sparred too, but that did not go too well either. He was beat by a brown belt, Dick Rainey out of San Antonio. Rainey got the first point, Trombley caught up, then Rainey got two points on a kick and beat him by one point. This was the end of Trombley's tournament days as a participant. From then on it was strictly his students that would take part.

Trombley always held two-night belt tests for advanced ranks, with several hours of material each night. Kurban would come to many of these tests, and one night told him that his tests were far too long, saying he should cut most of it. But Trombley refused. Once Trombley was at Kurban's dojo when a girl came into the office and said, "Master Kurban, I got 10 points." For every person they brought in, they would get points that could be used to get gear, or uniforms, etc. Of course, if Trombley ever complained to Karen about this, she would say "do you want to run your school your way or like Kurban?" And it was true, they may have been best friends, but they could not have been more different when it came to running a karate dojo.

Etiquette is something Americans do not always understand as it relates to what they see as a sport or hobby, despite wanting to learn it. This is particularly true of karate. One day a mother came into Trombley's dojo after the student's father signed up his son the day before. She saw her son bow to Trombley and her eyes got big. She came in the next day by herself and said her boy will never bow to anyone but God, so she pulled him out. It probably could have been explained to her that people have historically bowed for many reasons, but in the 1970's, anything "Oriental" was suspicious to some people. After that, Trombley added a section of his etiquette hand-out that gave an explanation about bowing as not a sign of subservience, but respect.

He started going to Kurban's dojo on Tuesdays and Thursdays. Kurban told him that students had to wear protective gear for sparring, which was somewhat new. Kurban brought out some yellow gear for Trombley to use that made him feel like a duck, but he used it anyway. When they sparred, Kurban was very nice to Trombley. He missed kicks on purpose, showing him a lot about tournament sparring. There were techniques Kurban used in his kicks that he did not learn in Okinawa. Kurban showed him how to chamber kicks for more power and speed. In Okinawa, people just picked their feet up and kicked, and groin strikes were not allowed. Students could kick to the legs, but not the groin. So, he learned to start wearing a cup. He knew a little about high kicks from sparring with Wendell Reeves at Jacksonville Beach, but Kurban taught him how to perform the kicks. He asked Kurban about stretching. Kurban did not need to stretch, but Trombley did.

These lessons with Kurban gave Trombley the idea to make another change to his system, high kicks. He decided to change the kicks in Gekisai Dai Ichi and Ni to go to the chin instead of the groin. In addition to high kicks, he wanted to make other changes. He wanted to add moves to the Gekisai katas, which turned out to be elements of the Hookiyu Katas that Toguchi created. He decided that he did not want to use the Hookiyu katas since they were too much like the Gekisai katas. One could say that this was the moment when Jay Trombley was officially out of Shoreikan Goju-Ryu and his own style, United Goju-Ryu was born. Changing katas without being the head of the system was just not done. He became the head of his own system instead.

Around this time, Trombley met Jim Choate, a man he would remain close with for the rest of his life. Choate was a lot like Trombley. He was rough around the edges, tough as nails who loved to fight, and had no problem telling people what he thought of them. Trombley loved this about Choate. Trombley met him at a Pat Burleson tournament in Fort Worth, downtown at a hotel (now the Omni). It was 1974 and Choate was a brown belt at the time, fighting another brown belt who had been doing well all day. During the fight, the two fighters collided at the same time and neither judge called a point. But Alan Steen, the head referee, stepped in and said he was calling a point for the other fighter (not Choate), saying, "I'm calling this myself." Choate got in Steen's face and yelled, "you can't do that!" The other officials got Burleson, who was Choate's instructor at the time, but Burleson really had nothing to say about it. Alan Steen had trained some of the biggest names in the business and everyone knew and respected him. Trombley had never seen anyone stand up to Steen before like that and was impressed. He introduced himself to Choate and they were friends from then on.

On one occasion Choate was coaching an all-star team representing Texas in an Oklahoma City tournament, run by Jim Butin. One of his heavyweights was unable to make it, so Choate was going to have to fight in his place. Choate had not fought since a tournament in Mexico City quite a while back, so he needed to train. He thought if he could spar with Roy Kurban for a while, he would do all right. Kurban was a well-known point fighter, so he would be good to practice with. Trombley set it up, and when Choate and Kurban started to spar, they went harder. Time went on and on. Trombley offered to keep time, but "forgot" to set the timer and the two fought with everything they had. Kurban finally piped up, "God dang Trombley, how much time left is there?" Trombley feigned surprise, "oh yeah, TIME!" Kurban was not really a street fighter but was a dynamite point fighter.

In College Station, Steve Powell threw a tournament. Tom Rieber and another student asked Trombley if they could do a Bunkai Kumite in a kata division. It had never been done before, a two-man kata, so to speak, but there would be more action and it might impress them. Joe Alvarado was the head referee and looked over at one judge, then the other, then walked over to Trombley and said they did not know how to judge it. He explained that it was offense and defense, same as kata. According to Trombley, Jim Choate was the only one to recognize what he was doing with kata kumite and kumite exercises. When he saw them doing it, he asked Trombley if he would teach some of it to him.

At one point Choate could not get any more rank from Burleson, who was his instructor. Burleson told Choate that he needed to do things for his community and have belt tests with the proceeds being donated to Burleson's organization. If Choate would bring him proof that he had done some of that, Burleson would consider it, but nothing ever came of it.

Trombley brought his students to as many tournaments as he could. He drove everyone who could fit in his van and most people from his schools attended and competed. By the mid-1990's, the focus of tournaments were completely about kids and a few adults who still collected trophies. Trombley knew why dojo owners threw them. When Trombley and Karen threw tournaments for the TKL (Traditional Karate League, something Trombley, Kurban, Rudy Smedley and others created), they made more money on food than anything else. Two students ran concessions and two of Karen's co-workers ran the front collecting tickets. It was very profitable, but a lot of work. When they enjoyed it, it was worth doing, but as time went on, they enjoyed it less and less.

Full Contact brought Trombley mentally back to Jacksonville Beach and it was separate from karate. Full Contact fighting was basically kickboxing, fighting to the knockout or decision. Rudy Smedley was someone Trombley was all set to train. He trained him one night and he never came back. He also trained Tom Rieber and Todd Kauffman. He supplied his fighters with orange juice, food, bandages, wraps, gauze, whatever they needed. The Traditional Karate League (TKL) organization he helped found also had a Full Contact branch, and fighters had to have a black belt before fighting at the professional level. This was something he did not agree with but went along with. Trombley thought if someone had talent, it should not matter what rank they were. But even in the regular tournaments, Trombley felt like the others did not treat his students in a fair manner. Brax Boyd, for example, would put Trombley's people against each other in sparring. He went to Kurban about this, and he said that is just how the computer put it out. This was a major factor in why Trombley eventually quit the TKL.

Back in those days everyone interested in martial arts wanted to be Bruce Lee or David Carradine from Kung Fu and learn what they saw in the movies and on tv. Inside the martial arts world, everything revolved around tournaments and demos. It was at one of these demos that Bruce Lee first got noticed in the 1960's, and Chuck Norris came from the point sparring matches, leading to his career in the movies as well. Most were not well known outside of martial arts, but there's no doubt Bruce Lee was a marketing spark. Trombley, in building his schools, wanted strong students who could compete. He wanted fighters. He trained full contact fighters in addition to karate. Sometimes his students did both, but most of the time he kept the two camps separate. His full contact fighters were on a strict diet and did separate drills from his karate students. But it did not really matter. Trombley trained all his students to fight hard and made sure his karate students did not solely train in point sparring.

In 1978 Trombley gave his first black to Alyce Strickland, and two years later he gave his second black belt to Tom Rieber, who, as a brown belt beat Tim Kirby, a black belt, in an amateur fight. Trombley gave him his belt in the ring after the fight. He gave Tom a Nidan rank unofficially when he came into the school off Pipeline and fought everybody. Much later, around 2005 Trombley asked him to come out to Ashley Oliver's black belt test. He then came back a few weeks later at Trombley's request and fought everybody in the school once again, despite not having trained in years.

Tom was the one who finally retired Trombley from sparring with students. Tom and Trombley had been sparring together since the apartment days. One night Tom hit Trombley with a right hook to the jaw, spinning him around. Trombley never saw it coming and after spinning around did not totally know where he was. Tom said, "Sensei, I'm back here." He could not let Tom know he was hurt so he mumbled something like, "now you know how to hit." He took off his gloves and never sparred again. He felt that if he ever showed weakness in front of his students, he would lose face. One night he was teaching students how to roll and as he went down, one leg hit the floor and he was in terrible pain, but he just kept talking, walking around trying to get it back to normal. But the worst injury was sparring with the famous fighter, Ronnie Ramsey. Ramsey connected with an axe kick to the top of Trombley's shoulder. He walked it off but had shoulder problems for the rest of his life.

In 1981, Trombley finally held an actual black belt test for two of his brown belts, Rusty Fralia and Todd Kauffman. At the same test, Shane Dodd and Shane Facemyer received junior black belts. Facemyer would go on to get his senior black belt a few years later with Lavada White. Facemyer and White were two deaf students that Trombley taught. This proved to be an interesting wrinkle since he had to use methods of teaching that relied less on talking and more on showing. Facemyer could read lips and sometimes he "spoke" to Lavada White for Trombley. During belt tests, the black belts at the panel started covering their mouths with their hands when they spoke to each other since Facemyer could tell what they were saying.

The Kauffman/Fralia test was the first actual black belt test. Alyce Strickland and Tom Rieber both received their black belts without the benefit of a test. The belt tests were a cumulative test with everything in the system the student knew being demonstrated, with sparring at the end. Because of this, sparring was never as quality as it was on a regular "fight night." At the end of a belt test, particularly a two-night test, the participants are designed to be completely exhausted by the time they got to the sparring portion of the test. For Fralia and Kauffman, Trombley invited acclaimed kickboxer Troy Dorsey and his two brothers, who were all Jim Choate's students at the time, to fight at the end of the test, making it especially difficult.

August 9. 1973

Thank you for your letter. I'm very glad to have been able to recieve your letter. Because the address you know where we lived 5 years ago. By the kindness of postman, I can recieve the letter.

I have been trip to around the world from February to July this year to teach Karate.

And so my reply to your letter ought to be late. If I know your address before, I could have been able to visit your Dojos. Now, we have 10 Dojoes in U.S.A. and set the U.S.A. headquarters in New York city.

You want to be the Branch Dojoes of my Shorei-kan which you wrote in your letter. Please let me know the details of your Dojoes. Maybe I permit you with great joy. Please comunicate Mr. Toshio Tamano who is chief instructor of the U.S.A. headquarters of Shorei-kan.

Please also get his permission. The address of u.s.a. headquaters is same one of the card enclosed.

I hope you all co-aporate and spread out the Shorei-kan Karate and Spirit all over the world. I have a plan to go to U.S.A. next year. I'm waiting for your reply.

Sincerly yours

Another letter from Seikichi Toguchi (1973)

Letter transcribed:

August 9, 1973

Thank you for your letter. I'm very glad to have been able to receive your letter. Because the address you know where we lived 5 years ago. By the kindness of postman, I can receive the letter.

I have been trip to around the world from February to July this year to teach karate.

And so my reply to your letter ought to be late. If I know your address before, I would have been able to visit your dojos. Now, we have 10 dojos in U.S.A. and set the U.S.A. headquarters in New York City.

You want to be the branch dojos of my Shorei-kan which you wrote in your letter. Please let me know the details of your dojos. Maybe I permit you with great joy. Please communicate Mr. Toshio Tamano who is chief instructor of the U.S.A. headquarters of Shorei-kan. Please also get his permission. The address of the U.S.A. headquarters is same one of the card enclosed.

I hope you all co-operate and spread out the Shorei-kan Karate and spirit all over the world. I have a plan to go to the U.S.A. next year. I'm waiting for your reply.

Sincerely Yours

Mr. and Mrs. Jay Trombley

Jay Trombley and his parents, Tucson Arizona

January 26, 1974

Greetings to all Shorei-Kan members,

I hope all is well with you in your dojo for the New Year. We here in New York City are doing very well, and Shorei-Kan is growing all the time.

I have received Shorei-Kan chestmarks which I will send to all branch dojos. The cost is $2.00 per patch plus 14¢ tax on each. I would appreciate it if you would order them in lots of 100. The total cost would be $214.00 including tax and shipping. I am selling them individually to my students at $2.50 each as a contribution to the workings of the dojo. You may use that as a guideline for your own students' purchases.

I am working on the completion of the Shorei-Kan Constitution which will better organize the dojos of Shorei-Kan Karate. I will mail you a copy of it when I have finished.

Master Toguchi, whom I saw this past month during my trip to Japan, is very well and sends all of you his very best wishes. He hopes to come to the U.S. and see us again soon. I hope to travel and visit all the Shorei-Kan dojos myself in the near future.

Until then, be healthy and practice hard.

Sincerely,

Toshio

Mr. Harvey Trombley
2005 S. W. Loop 820
Fort Worth, Texas 76134
U.S.A.

Tokyo,Feb. 2, 1977

Dear Mr. Trombley,

1 have duly received your letter of Jan. 3, 1977, for
which 1 thank you indeed, and 1 noted with pleasure that
you had completely recuperated now , and be back to
teaching Karate to your regular members at your dojo.

First of all, concerning U.S.A. headquaters, as you know,
Mr. Tamano used to be representative of SHOREI-KAN in
U.S.A., but now he is namely representative due to the
fact that he has not been active as representative.

Therefore, 1 would like to ask you to contact us directly
from now on.

By the way, 1 would like to inform you that old Okinawa
dojo, where you had studied in 1950's,was rebuilt in the
same place in 1976. As you may remember, my son. SEIKI is
now teaching Karate to many U.S. G.I.(American soldiers
stationed in Okinawa).

Finally speaking of my photos, 1 will send you one as
soon as available, which please be patient for a while.

With best regards to you.

Sincerely yours,

S. Toguchi

Letters from Shoreikan Headquarters in NY (1974) and one from Toguchi (1977)

Jay Trombley and Karen

Possum Kingdom Lake

91

Alyce Strickland, Black Belt #1 and Trombley, 1978

L to R: Trombley, Roy Kurban, Mike Ward, Jim Choate

Trombley and Tom Rieber, Black Belt #2

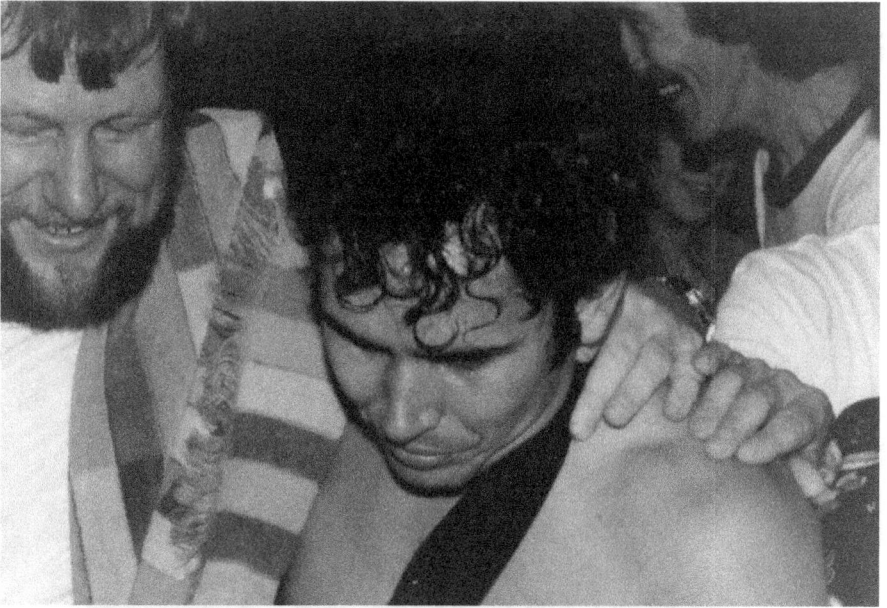

Tom Rieber after his fight with Tim Kirby where he received his black belt, 1980

L to R: Trombley, Chuck Norris, Tom Rieber

Trombley and Roy Kurban

Back Row L to R: Tom Rieber, David Kneer, Todd Kauffman
Front Row L to R: Rusty Fralia, Trombley, Shane Facemyer

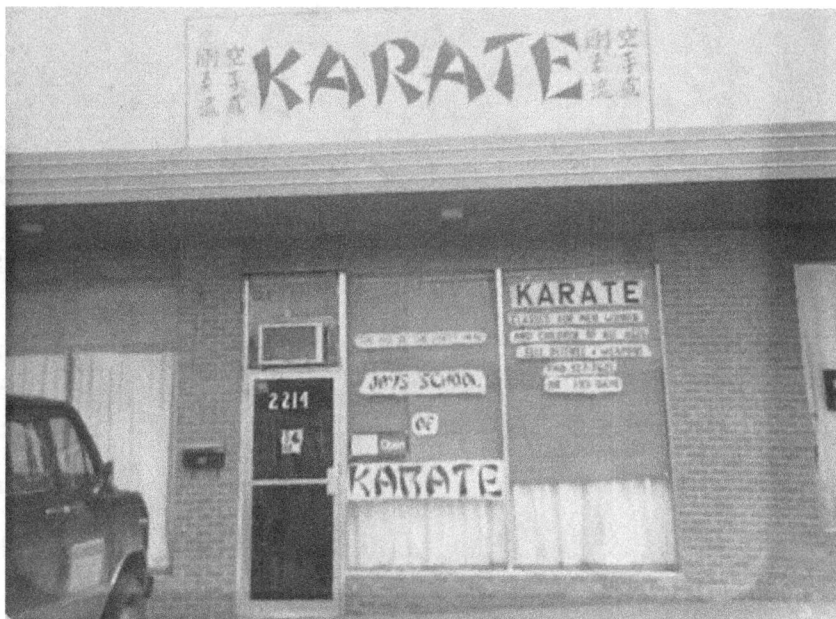

Dojo on McCart and Seminary, Fort Worth, Texas

Trombley in front of Dojo

Trombley and Karen

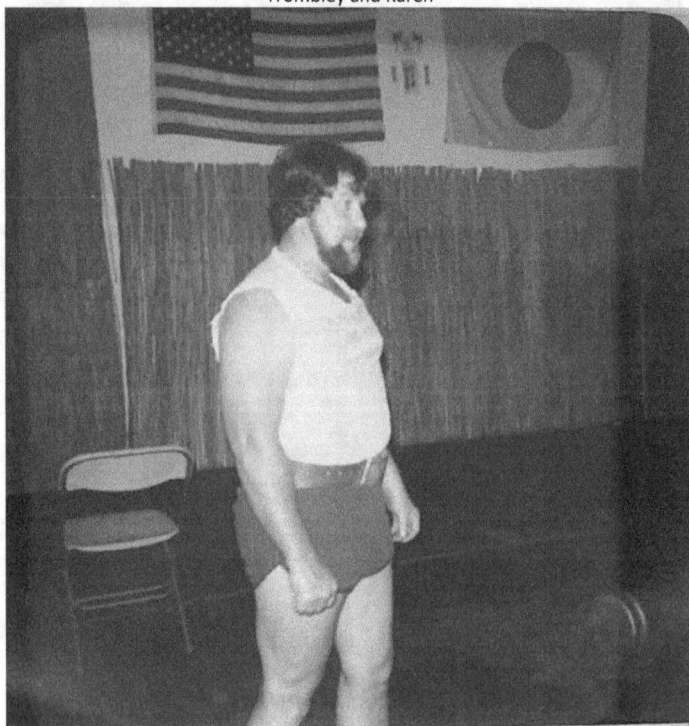

Trombley lifting weights at the dojo

Form D (Rev. 34)   License No. **1110**

Texas Boxing and Wrestling Law
Under Supervision of
Commissioner of Labor

MANAGER'S LICENSE

Issued to Jay Trombley

Address 2005 SW Loop 820, Fort Worth

Expires January 24, 1982

Not Transferable   Commissioner.

(Signature of Holder)

Jay Trombley

Rusty Fralia, Black Belt #3

Todd Kauffman, Black Belt #4

Trombley presenting a black belt to Rusty Fralia

Trombley and Lavada White, Black Belt #5

Trombley and Shane Facemyer, Black Belt #6

Trombley, Todd Kauffman, Bob Loewenstein on far right

Ronnie Ramsey and Trombley

Bill "Superfoot" Wallace and Karen Trombley

Todd Kauffman sparring with Tom Rieber, Jim Choate and Roy Kurban seated at belt panel

KARATE and LANGUAGE: The Vital Link

by Herm Nathan

Shane Facemyer and Lavada White, both deaf, throw in well-timed moves with feet and legs. Through lip-reading and signing, Shane has advanced at a remarkable pace.

Herm Nathan is a free-lance writer who resides in Grand Prairie, Texas.

Hands are very important in the life of Shane Facemyer.

Shane uses his hands—and feet—in karate, a sport in which fighting is synonymous with being fast as lightning. With one hand—chop! You could say karate is an honorable Oriental art.

Shane also uses his hands in another expressive manner. In signing—the language of the deaf.

Shane is deaf. He has been for all of his 12 years, but that hasn't stopped him from taking on karate and its amalgam of speed, agility and concentration. Shane is a first degree green belt.

The son of Thomas and Pauline Facemyer of Fort Worth, Texas, Shane is progressing hand-and-foot through his study of united goju-ryu, an Okinawan style of karate which puts equal emphasis on use of the hands and feet. For

Continued on page 42

Taking instruction from instructor Jay Trombley, Shane aspires to one day be an instructor himself. Shane communicates through karate as he does with his hands.

39

Article in the February 1980 edition of Black Belt Magazine about Trombley, Shane Facemyer and Lavada White

KARATE and LANGUAGE: The Vital Link

Continued from page 39

Surrounded by some of his trophies and ribbons, Shane's kata and fighting have won him many first place awards.

the past three years, he has been studying under the tutelage of Jay Trombley at his Karate Academy in Fort Worth.

At the recent annual Fort Worth National Pro-Am Karate Championship, Shane added another trophy to his 24 trophies and ribbons, most of them awarded for first place in kata (form) and fighting.

Shane found that a boy may be provoked in his young life into a bit of street-fighting, particularly, if he is a slight five foot four inches tall, 96 pounds and in the seventh grade. The fact that he is deaf usually won't bring much mercy from the average schoolyard bully. The taunting and laughing, and the pranks of thoughtless schoolmates, finally led Shane to Trombley's doorstep at the age of nine. One discouraged kid.

Shane explains his involvement with karate by saying, in signing, "It was something I wanted to learn for my self defense." As he embraced the art, he found it not only taught him self protection, but also self confidence in a world where those with impairments have to prove they are built Texas-tough.

Shane would like you to forget his deafness. He insists that he is "not deaf—just hard of hearing." But he is totally deaf, and yet, he compensates with what Jay Trombley describes as an uncanny sense of sound vibrations.

"He feels them through his body," said Trombley. "And he has developed such a sense of timing that found the kata concept, involving a series of co-ordinated steps and moves, "so easy, it's pathetic."

The physical side of the art also came easily to Shane, for as Trombley noted,

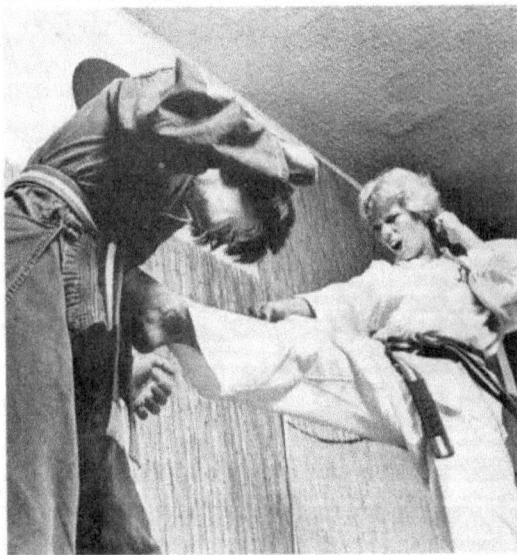

Top: Shane and Lavada converse in signing. Bottom: Shane, 12, and Rusty Fralia, 14, demonstrate muscular control unified with mental relaxation.

42

Shane uses his hands for karate—the all-encompassing means of self defense. Concentration and hard work may eventually earn Shane his black belt.

"He could already do the splits when he came in here. He came in here with loose hips. But he had to learn to go from one position to another and that was a little hard."

Trombley praises Shane as a quick learner. "He has advanced as much as a lot of kids I have taught for six to eight years. He catches on like a thoroughbred. Shane came in, and I told him it would be a long, hard road to karate.

But he has studied hard and has taken the same program as anyone else." Trombley would know as he began his study in Okinawa in 1955.

Shane would like to acquire the black belt and eventually teach, something he does already under Trombley's guidance. Trombley looks upon Shane's teaching at his school, both formally and informally, as part of his advancement process and learning how to communicate. "As far as I'm concerned, he speaks. We have no language barrier whatsoever," said Trombley.

Other barriers in Shane's life have come tumbling down since he took up the art. Said his mother, "With Shane at karate school, it has helped me with discipline problems. He was always superactive, but here he works so much of that out. It's wonderful to see the change the school has done for him."

Kid chops, kicks way up k

OOF! Instructor Jay Trombley gets the full impact of a kick from karate student Shane Dodd. Trombley considers the 8-year-old outstanding in the martial art and says he probably will have a black belt by the time he's a teenager. Photos by Mike Garrett.

By Vicky Kendig

While other kids spend their afternoons watching Superman and various TV heroes, Shane Dodd acts out his dreams in a karate studio.

The 8 - year - old, though shy and unassuming, has won trophies in all but one tournament he has entered since last fall.

His instructor, Jay Trombley, who teaches karate at 2214 W. Seminary, says Shane is an incredible student.

"He's very talented," Trombley says. "And of all the kids I've taught, I've never had one take it as seriously as he does."

Although instruction lasts for two hours three times a week, Trombley says Shane never has to be reminded to pay attention to spoken instruction or to do his exercises.

Karate is serious business for the third-grader.

His list of credits includes first place won at the Allen Steen's U. S. Karate Championship in Dallas last December; third place in "kata," or form, at November's Texas State Championship in Fort Worth and a first place in "kata" in the Texas World Open Pro Karate Championship in September at Waco.

In each, he was pitted against karate proponents of all ages in the form competition. In fighting, he competes only with those in his own age group.

The soft - spoken student is reluctant to brag about his conquests, but he says some of his school friends know he's taking karate and

think he's pretty lucky.

His favorite trophy, he says, is the one he was awarded in Dallas — because it's big and because it is the most important tournament he has entered.

In his white karate outfit and green belt, Shane looks a little like a miniature Bruce Lee — a flying ball of muscle — as he demonstrates a side snap kick to Trombley's chest.

When the Hurst Hills Elementary student began taking karate nearly two years ago, Trombley let Shane land kicks wherever he wanted on the 200 - pound instructor.

Now, it's a different story.

Shane's dad, Fort Worth policeman Gary Dodd, says at home at 616 Cranford Dr. in Hurst, Shane wants to demonstrate everything he has learned in class.

"He'd rather get in the floor and wrestle than anything else," Dodd says.

But sometimes it gets Dodd in trouble. Shane can hurt, he admits.

The karate student, however, never uses "hard" techniques — blows to vital areas — on his dad.

Trombley says he has taught Shane how to get out of a situation politely, or how to do it so it hurts.

He stresses to his young students not to brag about taking karate to their friends — or enemies.

Like a gunfighter with notches on his pistol, other kids might think a karate student is fair game for a fight.

Although the martial art is in-

(See Page 7)

FENDING A KICK from a trophy isn't Shane's objective. Competitors in tournaments where he gleaned these awards were real-life youngsters and adults intent on winning. The karate student has won trophies in three of four contests he has entered.

BAG AND BOY MEET as 8-year-old karate enthusiast Shane Dodd throws a side snap kick to the 65-pound bag. His prowess, gained over a two year period, is shown in his degree of karate — the first stage of a green belt—and the contests he has won. His goal: the coveted black belt.

Karate kid heads for black belt degree

(Starts on Page 1)

tended for self - defense, Shane's mother Shellà says she hoped karate would help build his self - confidence. "Self - defense was the last thing on my mind," she says.

Although she thought his interest might last a few months, his enthusiasm has not waned. "He's very serious about it. It's all business with him."

His room at home is draped with karate posters, and the latest karate magazines make up a good part of his reading.

A holder of the green belt first degree, Shane is looking forward to the next tournament, the Third Annual U.S. Tae - Kwan - Do Championship in Dallas March 26.

But his main goal is the highest degree in karate, the black belt.

He has moved through three degrees of the white, or beginning, belt and one of the green. He will have to go through four of the brown before reaching the ultimate category, which has nine degrees.

With obvious pride, Shane says Trombley has told him he probably will get the coveted black belt sometimes in his teens.

111

5 From Sensei to Shodai

As the 1980's continued, the school grew and grew. Eventually Trombley had two schools, one on McCart and Seminary (Fort Worth) and one in Hurst. There are too many students to mention during this time of constant tournaments and the Traditional Karate League (TKL). A red gi top was introduced as a prize at the end of the year for the student with the most tournament points accumulated. David Griffin was the next black belt after Shane Facemyer, then Ken Johnson. David and Ken became great friends and would become the top black belts of the school as students were coming and going. Alyce, Tom, Rusty, Todd, Shane, and Lavada had all left for a variety of reasons. People moved away, took jobs in other towns, or went off to college. Others just left and never came back. Some people had spouses who were tired of their karate spouse being at the dojo four or five nights a week and sometimes Saturdays. It was not a life that everyone could hold onto indefinitely, but luckily as people left, others came in. This would always be the case.

A few other changes were made during this time. A big one was that Jay Trombley would be called Shodai instead of Sensei. The system he created was indeed his own, and as black belts were being promoted, the head of the system needed a proper title and rank that only he could give. He became a 10th Dan with the title Shodai, meaning founder. When students lined up for class, they would be ten in a line before starting a new line, symbolizing Shodai's ten ranks of black belt.

Another change made to the system was the belts. Shodai had been using the same belt system he used in Okinawa, but it had several drawbacks. Depending on the rank, the student would receive a stripe and would have to sew it on his belt. The other issue was that when it came to tournaments, someone at 7th Kyu would look like a white belt, which was not the case. It was easier to change it and go with the colored rank system everyone else used.

	Original Belt System	Late 80's Belt Change
10th Kyu	White	White
9th Kyu	White with 1 green stripe	Gold
8th Kyu	White with 2 green stripes	Orange
7th Kyu	White with 1 wide green stripe	Purple
6th Kyu	Green with 1 white stripe	Green
5th Kyu	Green	Blue
4th Kyu	Green with 1 wide brown stripe	Red
3rd Kyu	Brown with 1 wide green stripe	Brown with 3 white stripes
2nd Kyu	Brown	Brown with 2 white stripes
1st Kyu	Brown with 1 wide black stripe	Brown
1st Dan	Black with 1 white stripe	Black with 1 white stripe

Another big event that happened in the 1980's besides Shodai's 35th Anniversary in the martial arts (October 1985) was the sword ceremony. Acquired by Charlie Clark, Sr. and paid for by his students, it was presented to Shodai as a traditional Japanese sword ceremony in the Japanese Gardens in Fort Worth. The Tatana has a 29-inch blade made by Osafune swordsmith Norimitsu 則光, son of Morimitsu 盛光. He worked from the Eikyo to the Kansho era (1429-65) of Japan. The sword was very special to Shodai, having come from his students as well as being a relic of ancient Japan. The next year, in 1986, he was awarded the Legion of Honor from Official Karate Magazine.

Bob Loewenstein was the next to receive his black belt. A close friend of Shodai, Bob built houses when he was not hanging out with Shodai or training at the dojo. He stayed with Shodai until 2003. Mark Ashraf and David Griffin's sister Sharon were next to get their black belts. Marshall Van Norden received his black belt from Shodai in 1989, but to this day remains the only black belt that Shodai rescinded after a very quick falling out. Shodai opened a dojo in the Val-Oaks Center in Hurst, where he would keep a school for the longest time of his career and moved into the last house he would ever reside in Bedford, down the street from the Val-Oaks dojo. The other dojos were closed, including a big one on Hurstview Drive nicknamed the "white elephant" because it was much bigger than he needed, and the cost reflected this waste. It contained a hot tub that Shodai eventually drained and filled up with rocks.

The dojo at Val-Oaks would see fourteen people get promoted to black belt, the highest number of black belts in the system. It contained a wood floor that the students help put down, sand, and screw down. It had a box frame underneath it with two by fours laid down sideways every few feet as support. When the floor wore out from wear, he put a new floor right on top of the old one, once again put together by Shodai and his students. This dojo had a giant hallway in the back where the heavy bags, focus pads, rubber knives, rubber guns, and clubs were all stored. There was also a bathroom, plus a girl's dressing room with a bathroom attached. In the main area the black belt dressing room was directly off the workout floor, and the boy's kyu rank dressing room was on the other side of it. Shodai's office was up front to the left when someone first walked in. The dojo had a tall ceiling that made electricity bills in the summer a complete nightmare, plus the back hallway area was poorly sealed, letting in outside air. Despite these issues, it was a perfect dojo in other ways. Nearly eight people could do the longest kata at the same time without fear of running into each other. The ceiling was high enough so that bo katas could be performed with absolutely no thought of damaging the ceiling. And six separate heavy bags could be hung at the same time.

The wave of black belts came in the 1990's: Allen Crowley, Christine Landmon, Andrew Smith, Marvin Madison, Kyle Brown, Russell Dare, Chris Collins, Jared Smith, and Ken Taliaferro. The original black belts had completely left by this time, so a new group was important for the dojo. Chris Collins received his junior black belt, then tested for his Shodan, like Rusty Fralia and Shane Facemyer had done before. Ken Taliaferro would be the first of Shodai's students to test for 5th Dan in 2007. Next was Alan Viengluang, the first junior black belt to test for Nidan at 17 years old.

Trombley wrote the following letter to one of his soon-to-be junior black belts. It serves as insight into what he felt it meant to become a Black Belt.

"From Sensei,

You know the rank of Shodan was a long way off when I started in Karate many years ago. At the time I had no idea how long the road would really be. But I knew if I was patient, and perhaps a little skilled, and tried to understand the way of the art, I might eventually make it to black belt.

I'm beyond Shodan now and I'm still working at it!

Promotion to Shodan in any martial art is a distinct honor. It means you have proficiency in the skill of the art. It means you are a person who should be respected and looked up to. It also means you've come a long way since those first unskilled moves, that indicated it was your first time in a dojo. But you managed to make it to the level you are now. You went through a lot of hard work and disappointments. But remember through a lot of love and understanding (because of your age) your instructor took you under his wing, talked to you, pushing you when you needed pushing, and offering you an open hand to help when you needed pulling. All the while he was watching you. I as your Sensei watched you from many vantage points based on my experience and training. On a practical level your last promotion was based on a performance test, competition, and your knowledge of the art.

Most martial arts have a code of ethics that serve as a guide for behavior. These are some of the things I thought you had, and some things I knew you could learn in deciding on your promotion.

As a Jr Black Belt you have a heavy load to carry until you reach Shodan.

As a Shodan you should be able to demonstrate self-confidence with humility. While you may be great at your art, there is no need to brag about it.

A second aspect of a Shodan is self-respect and tolerance. If you cannot respect yourself, it will be impossible to respect others or expect them to respect you.

Combined with self-respect is a tolerance for the ideas and ways of others. That tolerance allows you to accept students who may not have the knowledge or experience you have without belittling them.

One of the last items that went into my evaluation of your promotion, even before you stepped on the floor that day for your test, and that was my trust and faith in you. I had to believe in your potential in order to offer you such a promotion. I had to extend my trust and faith in you to line up to what I hoped and believed you could become. All of the other things are really unimportant if you cannot gain your trust and faith.

Before your mind is made up about your future in karate, it is probably wise to look back from whence you came. If you do not, when you get older you might regret it. The path or way you have been following is over X years old. So, before any path is to be followed you've got to answer this very important question: why did you get into the martial arts?

New students come into my school all the time and say, "I want to get my black belt." "Good," I say, "you've got a long way to go." There is nothing wrong with setting goals. Our society is filled with them. Studying to become a Shodan is an honorable goal. Very few make it. It's a lot of hard work.

However, if you stop reaching before you make it, you really haven't gone very far.

A Jr black belt is still in reality a high-ranking brown belt. Now as a Jr Black Belt you have to prove yourself able to compete at a black belt level.

Some people the ultimate goal is Shodan. Once they have it it's time to put the Gi (and the knowledge) in the closet and start something else. This type of person never should've made it. This attitude violates the entire philosophy of the martial arts and is a complete insult to that person's instructor, who extended his trust and faith in him. It is a way of stopping growth in the martial arts, and shortchanging yourself and others in the process you may be preventing growth. The past isn't lost, it's simply wasted.

If by chance you make it to Shodan and you see the promotion as a part of your growth you have come a long way. If you realized that you must give as well as receive in terms of helping others to learn your art, you have truly grown. Then you are more worthy of the rank you have worked for and received.

What's a black belt? There is, of course, the obvious answer. It's black, it's about 2 inches wide (1 7/8) and its in good or poor condition, depending on how long its been worn.

There are, however, other topics not worth discussing. For example, who is better, a boxer or a karate fighter? Could Chuck Norris beat Bruce Lee? How many bricks or boards can you break? And what was your answer? What talents do black belts actually possess?

* A black belt should possess undying courage
* A black belt should have great strength, because he has learned a way to generate power. In fact, he should have more power than he did before training.

* A black belt should know how to be humble because through training he should realize how much there is to learn, and how much he doesn't know.

* A black belt should realize that he has more to accomplish in his art.

* A black belt should know that he must earn respect from his students and his seniors. He can't demand it.

But a black belt cannot and should not be the tough guy on the block who wants to show off. Do not think you're invincible. You can be stopped.

When asked if you're a black belt, humbly but with pride say yes. But do not brag. A black belt should not automatically think he's the life of the party. He should not believe he will stay in shape for the rest of his life without continually working at it.

Never in public should a black belt criticize other black belts. Also, a black belt should not feel that others owe him something because he's a black belt.

We have all seen black belts who are conceited, braggarts, bullies, etc., but such people are not really black belts. Just because someone can kick or punch does not make him a black belt. A true black belt must have proper judgement before using his skill, since he is secure in his ability to handle any situation.

Now do not confuse bragging with confidence. Showing your ability isn't necessarily showing off. Performing a demonstration or showing off in a bar are totally different. In other words, we're dealing with a skill and most important pride. And perhaps that's what a major part of being a black belt is all about. pride.

It's one thing to use them in a self-defense situation where your life is in danger, but quite another to show off by bragging and telling everybody how great you are, and then pick a fight with a less competent person or student than you.

Keeping your word and telling another black belt you will do something is also an important part of your character. being on time for an appointment, whether for pleasure or business means being there 10 minutes early."

From Sensei,

You know the rank of shodan was a long way off when I started in Karate many years ago. At the time I had no idea how long the road would really be. But I knew if I was patient, and perhaps a little skilled, and tried to understand the way of the art, I might eventually make it to black belt.

I'm beyond shodan now and I'm still working at it!

Promotion to shodan in any martial art is a distinct honor. It means you have a proficiency in the skills of the art. It means you are a person who should be respected and looked up to. It also means you've come a long way since those first unskilled moves, that indicated it was your first time in a dojo. But you managed to make it to the level you are now. You went through a lot of hard work and disappointments. But remember through a lot of love and understanding (because of your age) your instructor took you under his wing, talked to you, pushing you when you needed pushing, and offering you a open hand to help when you needed pulling. All the while he was watching you. I as your sensei watched you from many vantage points based on my experience and training. On a practical level your last promotion was based on a performance test, competition, and your knowledge of the art.

Most Martial Arts have a code of ethics that serve as a guide for behavior. This is some of the things I thought you had, and some things I knew you could learn in deciding on your promotion.

As a JR Black Belt you have a heavy load to carry until you reach shodan

As a shodan you should be able to demonstrate self confidence with humility. While you may be great in your art, there is no need to brag about it.

A second aspect of a shodan is self-respect and tolerance. If you cannot respect yourself it will be impossible to respect others or expect them to respect you

Combined with self-respect is a tolerance for the ideas and ways of others. that tolerance allows you to accept students who may not have the knowledge or experience you do without belittling them.

One of the last items that went into my evaluation of your promotion, even before you stepped on the floor that day for your test, and that was my trust and faith in you. I had to believe in your potential in order to offer you such a promotion. I had to extend my trust and faith in you to live up to what I hoped and believed you could become. All of the others things are really unimportant if I cannot gain your trust and faith.

Before your mind is made up about your future in Karate, it is probably wise to look back from whence you came. If you don't, when you get older you might regret it. the path or way you have been following is over ____ years old. So before any path is to be followed you've got to answer this very important question: why did you get into the martial arts?

New students come into my school all the time and say "I want to get my black belt."

"Good," I say, "you've got a long way to go."
There is nothing wrong with setting goals. Our
society is filled with them. Studying to become
a Shodan is an honorable goal. Very few make
it. It's a lot of hard work.

However if you stop goal reaching before you
make it, you really haven't gone very far.

A 3R black belt is still in reality a high
ranking brown belt. Now as a 3R black belt
you have to prove yourself able to compete
on black belt level. ~~How many trophys~~
~~have you got under black belt? How many~~
~~have you got as a 3R black belt?~~

Some people the ultimate goal is Shodan.
Once they have it its time to put the gi
(and the knowledge) in the closet and start something else. This type of person never should've
made it. This attitude violates the entire philosophy
of the martial arts and is a complete insult to
that persons instructor, who extended his trust
and faith in ~~you~~ him. It is a way of stopping ~~your~~
growth in the martial arts, and short changing
yourself and others in the process. You may be
preventing growth. The past isn't lost, it's
simply wasted.

If by chance you make it to Shodan, you
see the promotion as a part of your growth, you
have come a long way. If you realized that you
must give as well as recieve in terms of helping
others to learn your art, you have truly grown.
Then you are more worthy of the rank you have
worked for and recieved.

Whats a black belt? There is, of course, the ~~time~~ obvious answer. Its black, its about 2 inches wide (1 7/8) and its in good or poor condition, depending on how long its been worn.

There are, however, other topics not worth discussing. For example, who is better, a boxer or a Karate fighter? Could Chuck Norris beat Bruce Lee? How many bricks or boards can you break? And what was your answer?

What talents do black belts actually possess?

- A black belt should possess undying courage.
- A black belt should have great strength, because he has learned a way to generate power. In fact, he should have more power than he had before training.
- A black belt should know how to be humble because through training he should realize how much there is to learn, and how much he doesn't know.
- A black belt should realize that he has more to accomplish in his art.
- A black belt should know that he must earn respect from his students and his seniors. He cant demand it.

But a black belt cannot and should not be the tough guy on the block who wants to show off. Dont think your invincible, you can be stopped.

When asked if your a black belt humbley but with pride say yes. But dant brag.

A black belt shouldnt automatically think he's the life of the party. He shouldnt believe he will stay in shape for the rest of his life without continually working at it.

Never in public should a black belt critique other black belts. Also a black belt shouldn't feel that others owe him something because he's a black belt.

We have all seen black belts who are conceited, braggarts, bullies, etc., but such people are not really black belts. Just because someone can kick or punch does not make him a black belt. A true black belt must have proper judgement before using his skill, since he is secure in his ability to handle any situation.

Now don't confuse bragging with confidence. Showing your ability isn't necessarily showing off. Performing a demonstration or showing off in a bar, are totally different. In other words, were dealing with skill & most important pride. And perhaps that's what a major part of being a black belt is all about. Pride

Its one thing to use them in a self-defense situation where your life is in danger, but quite another to show off by bragging and telling everybody how great you are, and then pick a fight with a less competant person or student that̲h̲a̲n̲ you.

Keeping your word and telling other Black Belts you will do something is also a important part of your ~~character~~. Being on time for an appointment, weather for pleasure or business means being t̲h̲e̲r̲e̲ 10 min early.

The following note was something Trombley copied down that helped illustrate his feelings about giving things away for free, particularly paying dues:

Master/Teacher made This point To his sTudenT, Who Thought he Knew enough, So he sTill WanTed To Train, BuT NoT PAY.

You Know sTudenT;
When you GIVE something To a man or do Something For him (Free) The First Time he Will hug you and shake your hand;
Second Time he Takes his haT off;
Third Time he bows,
ForTh Time he yawns,
FifTh Time he Nods
SixTh Time he insulTs you;
And The SevenTh Time he Sue's you For noT giving him enough.
You Know sTudenT; We musT pay For everyThing ThaT We receive From our Senses.

Dear Mr. Harvey Jay Trombley

Jan. 25, 1984

I have duly received your letter of Nov 9, 1983,
for which I thank you indeed.

First of all, I noted your letter's content, and
very pleased to know that you have been
active in karate for many years.

I have been teaching the true spirit of Shorei-
Kan, and had visited Canada to instruct Shorei-
Kan Karate in 1982.

I would like to inform you that there is the
U.S.A headquarter following, so please contact
Mr. Ichiro Naito.

Mr. Ichiro Naito
372 CENTRAL PARK WEST APT 7.5 NEW YORK
N.Y. 10025 U.S.A. TEL (212)222-1159

Yours truly

H. Maeda
for Master Toguchi

125

Mr. Harvey Trombley
2005 S.W. Loop 820
Fort Worth Texas
76134 U.S.A.
DEAR SIRS:

We would like to inform that our master. Seikichi Toguchi
will make a trip to U.S.A. and Canada detailing as under,
therefore, we want you to contact our master during his
stay in U.S.A. and Canada

S C H E D U L E

DEPARTURE OF JAPAN:JULY 27,1985
ARRIVAL OF NEW YORK: JULY 27,1985

DEPARTURE OF NEW YORK: AUGUST 14,1985
ARRIVAL OF TORONTO : AUGUST 14,1985

DAPARTURE OF TORONTO: AUGUST 30,1985
ARRIVAL OF JAPAN: AUGUST 30,1985

Master. Seikichi Toguchi will stay at Mr. Scott Lenzi
Shorei-Kan Okinawan Goju-Ryu 2 Reynolds Lane Buchanan,
N.Y. 10511 U.S.A. Tel from July 27,1985 to
August 14,1985. and at Mr.Tomoaki Koyabu Shorei-Kan
Canada Headquaters Cheif Instructor 1324 East 6th
Avenue, Vancouver, B.C. Canada V5N 1pl Canada Tel:
(604)874-5785.

We want you to contact the above, and if you have time,
please get his Karate instruaction.

Sincerely yours.

                                        For Master. Seikichi Toguchi

More Letters from Seikichi Toguchi's Representatives

Jay Trombley's Karate
2214 W. Seminary
Ft. Worth, TX 76115

J. TROMBLEY'S KARATE
453 BEDFORD EULESS RD.
HURST, TX 76053

JAY TROMBLEY

Jay Trombley is one of a few karateka who has the courage of his own convictions. His ideals are not the only ones acceptable in the martial arts, but he speaks out for what he believes in and refuses to compromise his ideals in order to receive recognition.

Jay has been a promoter and teacher for over thirty years. A native New Hampshire son, Jay came to the Ft. Worth area and has been a leader of quality martial arts for 30 years.

In a recent ceremony at the Japanese Gardens in Ft. Worth, Jay was presented with a 450-year-old signed and dated samurai sword in recognition for his work in the arts. His friends Ray Kurban, Larry Caster, and Jim Choate were there with his students to honor him.

Jay has been a promoter of tournaments and full contact, putting together the Alvin Prouder vs. Billye Jackson fight. His greatest pleasure is in working with his students.

For his dedication, honesty, and service in the martial arts, Jay is awarded the "Legion of Honor" from OFFICIAL KARATE Magazine.

Official Karate Legion of Honor Award, 1986

OFFICIAL KARATE'S

LEGION OF HONOR

1986

JAY TROMBLEY

Jay Trombley is one of a few karateka who has the courage of his own convictions. His ideals are not only ones acceptable in the maritial arts, but he speaks out for what he believes in and refuses to compromise his ideals in order to receive recognition.

Jay has been a promoter and teacher for over thirty years. A native Vermont son, Jay came to the Ft. Worth area and has been a leader of quality martial arts for 30 years.

In a recent ceremony at the Japanese Gardens in Ft. Worth, Jay was presented with a 450-year-old signed and dated samurai sword in recognition for his work in the arts. His friends Roy Kurban, Larry Caster, and Jim Choate were there with his students to honor him.

Jay has been a promoter of tournaments and full contact, putting together the Alvin Prouder vs. Billye Jackson fight. His greatest pleasure is in working with his students.

For his dedication, honesty, and service in the martial arts, Jay is awarded the "Legion of Honor" from OFFICIAL KARATE Magazine.

Sword Ceremony when students gave Shodai a Samurai sword dated 1600's
L to R: Rusty Fralia, Shodai, Ken Johnson, David Griffin, Lavada White

Senior Student Rusty Fralia presents the antique Samurai sword to Shodai

Shodai and Sword

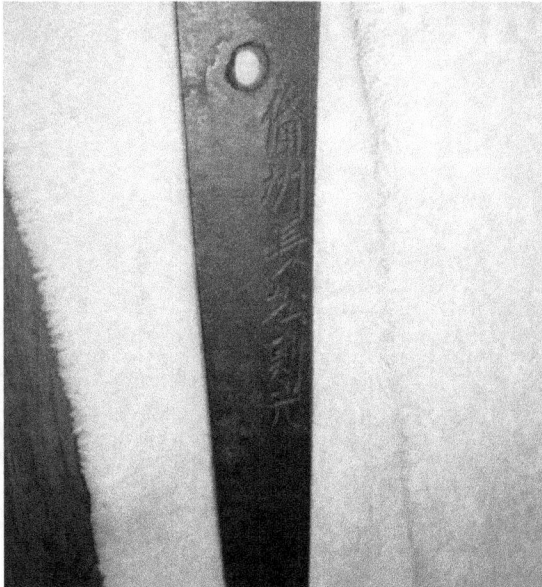

Signed Handle of Shodai's Osafune Norimitsu Sword

Shodai and Karen

中國海灘
CHINA BEACH
SINCE GOLD RUSH TIMES, THIS
COVE WAS USED AS A CAMPSITE
BY MANY OF THE CHINESE
FISHERMEN WHO WORKED IN
AND AROUND SAN FRANCISCO
BAY. THEIR EFFORTS TO SUPPLY
THE NEEDS OF A YOUNG CITY
HELPED ESTABLISH ONE OF
THE AREA'S MOST IMPORTANT
INDUSTRIES AND TRADITIONS.

Belt Panel: L to R: David Griffin, Lavada White, Shodai, Rusty Fralia

Shodai and Karen, Rusty Fralia just off camera – 30th Anniversary in the Martial Arts, 1985

IN HONOR OF
SHODAI
FOR 30 YEARS DEDICATION
TO THE MARTIAL ARTS

Locals do well in Arlington karate tourney

By TRISHIA JACOBS
Special to the News

ARLINGTON — Jay Trombley's Karate Academy of Hurst had 16 entrants in the annual Arlington Invitational Karate Championships Saturday at the Woodland West Recreation Center. And despite the lesser numbers than some of the other clubs, Trombley's came within one point of the team championship.

It was standing room only as spectators and 155 participants from Dallas-Fort Worth, Denton, Sherman, DeSoto, Austin, Bryan and Alexandria, La., crowded into the gymnasium to watch 5-year-olds and up compete for trophies in 11 divisions in for (kata) and fighting.

The annual event is sponsored by Roy Kurban and the American Black Belt Academy of Arlington to allow karate enthusiasts the opportunity to support the community and share in the Christmas spirit.

The proceeds from last year's tournament went to a local shelter for battered and abused women. This year they money will go to Wish With Wings, an organization formed by one of Kurban's former students, Pat Snggs.

With for Wings's purpose is to grant wishes for terminally ill children 12-year-old Jennifer Malloy of Chicago. She has a rare form of cancer, but had to undergo three operations. Malloy loves the martial arts and actually found an isolated half-

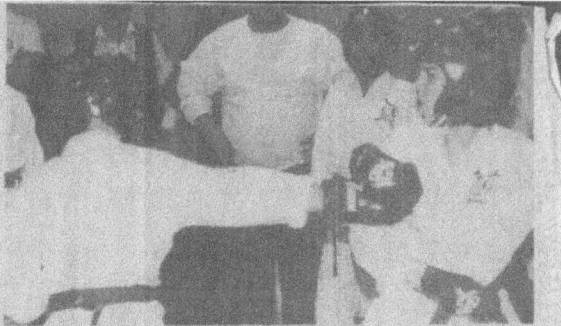

way at the hospital to practice her katas, oblivious to the tubes, wires and IVs.

It is her wish to fly to California and meet pro wrestler Holk Hogan, which the tournament will help pay for.

The Hurst-Euless-Bedford area was well represented by Trombley's school. Kenneth Johnson won the grand champion fighting trophy and also placed first in the black belt men's form (kata) division. This is the second year that the 21-year-old Sensei (instructor) has won the fighting division

with Goju-ryu karate style.

Mark Ashraf placed second in the form division and third in fighting. He is also a black belt.

Sharon Griffin, a brown belt, placed first in both women's divisions in fighting and form.

Others from Trombley's to carry away trophies were Jay Clark, Mario Molina, Ashley Fischer, Scott Wolf, Andrew Smith, Dan Tinker, Glen Cunningham, Gregg Haffner, Steve Tinker, Toby Shedhe, Dan Trang, Anos Lewis, Arthur Gams and Richard Wolf.

TRISHIA JACOBS

Ashley Fischer, left, blocks a move by her opponent during the Arlington Invitational Karate Championships Saturday at the Woodland West Recreation Center in Arlington. Fischer was one of several members of Jay Trombley's Karate Academy of Hurst to bring home a trophy.

JAY TROMBLEY'S 1ST ANNUAL U.G.J.K.A.

UNITED GOJU KARATE ASSOCIATION

SUMMER NATIONAL KARATE CHAMPIONSHIPS

AUGUST 17, 1985
EULESS JUNIOR HIGH
FORT WORTH, TEXAS

SANCTIONED BY A.O.K. & U.G.J.K.A.
AN "A" RATED, TRIPLE POINT EVENT
RATED BY "KARATE ILLUSTRATED"

PRODUCED BY: JAY & KAREN TROMBLEY
DIRECTED BY: ROY KURBAN & JIM CHOATE

GOOD TIMES VAN PRESENTS

ALL STAR PROFESSIONAL KICKBOXING

Photo by Steve Anderson

SATURDAY, OCTOBER 17, 1987 **PROGRAM** BILLY BOB'S COWTOWN COLISEUM

Jay Trombley/Promoter

Jay Trombley began his martial arts career in Okinawa in 1955. His marine corps assignment to force recon kept him in Okinawa for a five year tour of duty. When Jay Trombley was not performing his chores for the corps, he was involved in five hour training sessions in traditional Goju karate under world reknown Master Seikichi Toguchi, and was the first American to receive a black belt from the master. Mr. Trombley's area of expertise in Okinawan martial arts systems also includes a thorough schooling in weaponry which he acquired from Hohan Soken.

Jay Trombley began teaching karate to marines and members of the navy's elite U.D.T. teams shortly before his discharge in 1960. He has been teaching karate continuously for over twenty-eight years. Jay has worked with navy, marine, air force personnel, and several law enforcement agencies. He has a solid boxing background having operated a professional boxing gym in the past. He has trained literally thousands of students in United Goju karate as well as working with such excellent kick boxers as world ranked Glen McMorris.

Jay has worked as a judge in national and international bouts. Jay Trombley's wonderful wife Karen enjoys all aspects of the martial arts and is one of the sport's most enthusiastic fans!

138

ALL STAR PROFESSIONAL
KICK
BOXING
★ ★ RINGSIDE SEAT ★ ★
$22
SATURDAY, OCTOBER 17, 7:30 P.M.
BILLY BOB'S COWTOWN COLISEUM

David Griffin, Black Belt #7

Ken Johnson, Black Belt #8

Bob Loewenstein, Black Belt #9

Mark Ashraf, Black Belt #10

Shodai and Sharon Griffin, Black Belt #11

Allen Crowley, Black Belt #12

Christine Landmon, Black Belt #14

Kyle Brown, Black Belt #15

Andrew Smith, Black Belt #16

Marvin Madison, Black Belt #17

Russell Dare, Black Belt #18

144

Chris Collins, Black Belt #19

Ken Taliaferro, Black Belt #20

145

Jarred Smith, Black Belt #21

Alan Viengluang, Black Belt #22

The Hurst Dojo on Pipeline

Shodai and students

L to R: Ken Johnson, David Griffin, Lavada White, Shodai, Rusty Fralia

Shodai and students

Russell Dare and Shodai

Kyle Brown and Shodai

Shodai and David Griffin

Chris Landmon and Shodai

Allen Crowley and Shodai

Shodai and Lavada White

Shodai and Mark Ashraf

L to R: Chris Collins, Marvin Madison, Ken Taliaferro, Shodai (seated), Jared Smith, Bob Loewenstein, Alan Viengluang (seated)

L to R: Ken Taliaferro, Chris Collins, Marvin Madison, Jarred Smith, Alan Viengluang

Roy Kurban's
American Black Belt Academy
proudly presents the 1994

FORT WORTH
INVITATIONAL
KARATE CHAMPIONSHIPS

Saturday, October 8, 1994
Tarrant County Convention Center

Sanctioned by the
TRADITIONAL KARATE LEAGUE

Jay Trombley

Jay Trombley began his martial arts training while stationed in Okinawa with the U.S. Marine Corps in 1955. Through the fortuitous intercession of Sgt. Joe White, Jay was introduced to Master Seguchi Toguchi and began his lifelong study of Goju Ryu karate.

The training in the Okinawan Dojo was brutal. And many Marines withdrew from the classes. Mr. Trombley embraced this opportunity of a lifetime and committed himself to five years of focused practice.

While training under Master Toguchi, Mr. Trombley was provided the opportunity to train under legendary weapons expert Master Hohan Soken.

Upon conclusion of his tour with the Marine Corps, Sensei Trombley knew that he wanted to teach karate and made a lifelong commitment to a teaching career which has spanned three decades.

In addition to teaching, he was nationally recognized as an excellent official of tournament and kickboxing events, a promoter of tournaments and world championship kickboxing matches, and trainer of kickboxing champions. In recognition of these achievements, *Official Karate Magazine* inducted Jay Trombley into the martial arts' Legion of Honor.

Shodai Jay Trombley's life is a tribute to United Goju Ryu, the Traditional Karate League and the martial arts world.

Brax Boyd has enjoyed an outstanding and diversified sports and fitness career which has included excellence in many different sports including football on the collegiate level at the University of Texas at Arlington in the early 1970's.

With a strong background in peak sports conditioning methods including weight lifting, management of newly-introduced Nautilus clinics in the mid-1970's, and overall competition skills on many levels, Mr. Boyd began his study of Taekwondo and earned his first degree black belt in 1977.

In addition to martial arts instructor skills, he earned his masters degree in 1987 in political science and later his PhD in higher education administration at the University of North Texas. He presently serves as an adjunct faculty member in political science at both Tarrant County Junior College and Cedar Valley College.

Today Mr. Boyd is a 4th degree black belt and has operated his Grand Prairie Karate Academy since 1984.

He has coached many of his students to championship levels in TKL competition.

The Grand Prairie Karate Academy is consistently among the top martial arts schools in TKL tournament competition each year and hosts one of the league's top-producing, well-managed and enjoyable annual competitions, the TKL Grand Prairie Invitational in the spring.

Shodai on his 45th Anniversary in the Martial Arts, 2000

6 Full Circle

By the end of the 1990's, Shodai abandoned the tournament world and concentrated solely on running his dojo in Hurst, Texas. By this time, his karate students learned full contact training drills but continued to spar both iri kumi (continuous free-style sparring) along with point sparring. It would not take long for Shodai's method of training people to spar to be outdated. The contact allowed in tournament point sparring was getting lighter and lighter, despite the gear students had to wear. Wearing protective gear allowed tournament fighters to make hard contact, which had been debated ever since protective equipment began. Next to go was groin contact. Still, Shodai continued to train his students with both hard contact and with groin strikes allowed. It did not matter, though, since his students stopped going to tournaments entirely, with one or two rare exceptions. But Shodai still had his dojo, and it was thriving.

In 2002, Trent Boe, Mike Perry, and Brodie Wolgamott all tested together to replenish the ranks after the middle guard of the 1990's black belts were all but gone. But soon Collins and Loewenstein both left, leaving Taliaferro, Marvin Madison, Boe, Perry, and Wolgamott.

Then in 2003, Shodai made the biggest change to the system since changing his title to Shodai, and that was changed the name of his karate system to Ketsugo Goju-Ryu, the Japanese word for United being "Ketsugo." The name was changed when Shodai's Okinawan student Emi, who had received candy from Marines when she was little Okinawan girl in the 1950's, helped Shodai with some translations. The black belt patch would be changed from the Gogen Yamaguchi fist to a chrysanthemum design that was more in line with Toguchi's Shoreikan patch. The kyu rank patch underwent a few transformations to the current style of a bamboo outline, the receptive heavens and creative earth symbol from the I-Ching, the two kanji for Karate, the letters KGJKA (for Ketsugo Goju-Ryu Karate Association) and the black belt patch inside.

Very little changed in the system after that, a few moves here and there, but nothing too dramatic. Shodai changed the 5th counter in Kumite San, the 4th and 5th counters in Kumite Shi, things like that. In 2005, Ashley Oliver, who had taken karate from Shodai as a teenager in the 1980's, received her black belt, then in 2007, her husband Robert Oliver received his black belt. This would be the last black belt given at the Val-Oaks Hurst dojo.

Later in 2007, Shodai closed the school in Hurst. He moved his equipment, bamboo walls, heavy bags, inventory, the nafudakake, and his scroll from Okinawa, and opened his last dojo in Watauga, Texas. Starting over in Watauga was made easier by having several black belts to start with. He signed up two new students right away and things were on their way. The dojo was off Rufe Snow Drive, which had heavy traffic going north and south. The exposure was immense compared to the dojo in Hurst. Sadly, in 2009, Shodai's old friend Bob Loewenstein would die of cancer on Thursday, November 26th. He was sixty-two years old.

Over the coming years, Shodai promoted two more people to Shodan, George Eastlick and Cliff Knudson. Knudson had been a junior black belt under Shodai but left when he was a young teenager. He went through the entire system twice, once as a kid, then again as an adult. Shodai had promoted other junior black belts, but if they left, they usually never came back to get their senior black belt, until Cliff.

Many people came and went to the Watauga school. David Griffin came back to Shodai there and many black belt visitors came in, like Sharon Griffin and Lavada White. Chris Landmon left a while back but always made it to the black belt tests. As time went on, more people left than came in. First Taliaferro, then Perry, Ashley Oliver, Wolgamott, Eastlick, then Griffin. By the end, Cliff Knudson and Robert Oliver were the only active black belts left.

On March 26, 2016, Shodai closed his Watauga dojo, retiring from karate. He never liked the Watauga dojo and always spoke poorly of it. It had industrial carpet in it, which he always intended to change to hard wood, but never really wanted to spend the money on it. There were a lot of students in Watauga, but it was not more than a year or two into his lease that the City of Watauga disallowed the use of temporary street sign advertisement, which really helped draw students to the school. After that, he was lucky to get one student a month, and most students never stayed more than a few months anyway. Times were changing. Shodai was fully out of the tournament scene, and he felt like people were getting softer and softer with each passing year. By 2016, he was down to only a handful of students. This took a toll on him both mentally and physically. Gone were the days that he would exercise or work on katas during the day. He still loved karate, but he was losing interest in the present. He longed for the old days and was ready to retire.

Being the highest black belt in the system, in the fall of 2016 Shodai officially transferred the system to Robert Oliver (the author) in a ceremony conducted at Robert's dojo, Oliver Karate Academy, in Bedford, Texas. Shodai left on his own terms and did exactly what he wanted to do, as usual. Shodai continued to visit Robert's dojo on the weekends, sometimes to watch class, but most of the time he and Karen came into the office to visit and reminisce. Shodai said that once in his McCart and Seminary dojo, a school bus driver came in after seeing Shodai doing a kata through the window. He asked if that was what karate is and Shodai said yes, and a whole lot more.

Two people who made brown belt under Shodai but came back after he retired was Tim Bryant and Armando Navarro. Tim started karate in 2001 but left as a 1st kyu brown belt in 2006 after he got married. Armando made it to brown belt under Shodai in the Hurst dojo but left as well. Tim enrolled at Robert Oliver's KGJKA dojo after Shodai retired, and shortly after, Armando joined as well. When he came back with Tim Bryant, they trained together and made black belt under Robert Oliver, but Shodai was present for the test and signed both of their certificates. On their way home from that belt test, Shodai told Karen that he finally felt like his system was going to carry on.

Shodai died on November 23rd, 2022, at the age of eighty-four, after battling kidney failure for several months. He was diagnosed with diabetes years earlier but did not take care of it like he should have. He stayed away from sugar and never drank alcohol, but apart from that he took care of himself by lifting weights, doing karate, and drinking water. He ate what he wanted, but he mostly paid attention to his body. He had back problems that kept him in pain for days at a time. By the end he was only sporadically coherent. Sometimes he could barely talk, and other times he sounded like his old self. It was hard to watch, and Karen bore the brunt of it all. To that end his death was a relief. He was ready and eventually his body and mind cooperated.

He left behind a karate system that is uniquely his. It is a combination of 1950's era Shoreikan Goju-Ryu Karate and traditional Okinawan weapons, American boxing, jiu jitsu self-defense, and Tae Kwon Do kicks. He also left behind his friendship and his love. But Shodai was no saint. He probably upset more people than he endeared himself to. A lot of that was because he refused to do anything but speak his mind. He had no interest in sugar coating anything or playing politics with people that could have really helped him. His friendship meant he could say whatever he wanted and to be his friend was to accept that. But his loyalty was like the girl in Okinawa with the apple. If he gave his karate to you, he was giving of himself and he wanted you to understand what it meant for him to give it to you.

Author's note: Shodai repeated many of the same stories he always told, about Okinawa, old schools he used to have, former students, stories about the full contact days, his childhood, you name it. Sometimes I heard stories I never heard, moves in the system, etc. One thing about people, when they tell stories, they vary from time to time depending on their mood, the time of day or the audience. Occasionally Karen would chime in and correct Shodai on a date or a name, maybe going back and forth trying to remember certain details. Shodai often said, "if Bob (Loewenstein) were here, he'd remember who that was."

The information in these chapters has been taken from stories and conversations I had with Shodai over the years, copying down things he told me. Naturally people remember things differently; people make mistakes in what they remember. I was lucky enough to receive some contributions from a few prior students and I have put them here. If there were any inconsistencies, I left them as is.

One more note: Brodie Wolgamott, Shodai's 25th Black Belt, died July 11th, 2021, at the age of 50 after sustaining injuries from a motorcycle accident. I knew Brodie before he was a student with Shodai, and it was a complete coincidence the first time I saw him at the dojo right before his black belt test. I had not seen him in years, and when I saw him there, I could tell he was a different person, more focused, but still funny as hell. He was always known for being impossible to hurt. Once at a party a stereo speaker fell onto his head. He just looked at it, then went on like nothing happened. As a karate instructor his gift was the ability to spar with people of whatever rank they were. He had an internal gauge that just knew how hard he should spar with someone. It was remarkable and something I always tried to imitate. He was a great person, and everyone loved having him at the dojo.

Trent Boe, Black Belt #23

Mike Perry, Black Belt #24

Brodie Wolgamott, Black Belt #25

Ashley Oliver, Black Belt #26

The author, Black Belt #27

Shodai at Jim Choate's 7th Dan Belt Test with Pat Burleson

Shodai with Ishmael Robles

Shodai with Jim Choate

Ashley Oliver and Shodai

L to R: Lavada White, Tom Rieber, David Griffin, Ashley Oliver, Brodie Wolgamott, Shodai, Chris Landmon, Mike Perry, Ken Taliaferro

Back Row L to R: the author, Ashley Oliver, Mike Perry
Front Row L to R: Brodie Wolgamott, Shodai, Ken Taliaferro

L to R: Ashley Oliver, the author, Shodai, David Griffin, Brodie Wolgamott

George Eastlick, Black Belt #28

Cliff Knudson, Black Belt #29

Karen and Shodai – 55th Anniversary in the Martial Arts, 2010

L to R: George Eastlick, Ashley Oliver, Shodai, David Griffin, the author

L to R: Ashley Oliver, the author, Shodai, Cliff Knudson, David Griffin

Shodai and the author, Shodai's Official Retirement, 2016

Ashley Oliver, Shodai, and the author

L to R: Armando Navarro, Shodai, the author, and Tim Bryant, 2018

L to R: Cliff Knudson, Brodie Wolgamott, Ashley Oliver, Armando Navarro, Shodai, the author, Tim Bryant, David Griffin, 2018

Tim Bryant, Black Belt #30

Armando Navarro, Black Belt #31

The Honbu Dojo for Ketsugo Goju-Ryu Karate, Colorado Springs, 2022

7 Stories from the Dojo

Author's note: for many of these stories, I have changed the names of the participants out of respect and privacy.

Shodai told stories all the time, usually at night after class was over. Depending on who was there, he might tell a story about something in Okinawa that would remind him of someone else, which would remind him of something that happened in another dojo, and so on. Sometimes it was hard to keep it all straight, and the stories might change slightly. There was usually a point to the story, a lesson he wanted us to get without telling us directly. For example, if he talked about how someone bragged about himself all the time, he was telling you not to brag about yourself. He wanted his students to examine themselves. And he tested people. He might say, "do you remember me telling you about the founder of Isshin-Ryu?" Tatsuo Shimabuku had better fall out of that person's mouth quickly.

At other times his stories were purely for entertainment.

Self-Defense

One day Roy Kurban, Jim Choate, and Shodai were sitting around and Shodai said, "let's do some self-defense." He said they would take turns doing a hold or something, and each person would show what they would do. The other guys were not too sure about self-defense for holds. Choate could fight for sure, and Kurban was one of the best point fighters in Texas, but neither one had self-defense moves they could teach their students. This was not unusual since most dojos were designed for tournaments, which meant kata and sparring only. When Kurban was ready to put self-defense in his system, he came to Shodai.

Fred

A man walked in, bowed to the front of the dojo, then to Shodai. He said his name was Fred. He had a dojo close by on Seminary Dr in Fort Worth, and his style was Shorinji Ryu. He just wanted to come down and say hello and say that he was teaching in a school down the way and Shodai could come see him some time. Later Shodai went to visit him and the first thing he noticed was a big tiger head on the window, a Shotokan symbol, not known for Shorinji Ryu, which was not a huge deal, but a detail Shodai felt like this person should have been aware of. After walking in, Shodai saw a set of steps leading up to an office. Fred was there and said to come on up. They talked and he noticed Fred was smart with karate terminology, but Shodai really wanted to see a workout. He asked him what time class started. Fred tried to dissuade him and said, "you don't want to see this class, they're just beginners." Shodai said no, when he went into a martial arts school, he liked to see the beginners, because the beginners reflect the instructor. He said if he saw a basic class, he would know more about what he was about. But since he really did not want Shodai to see the class, Shodai left. But instead of going back to his dojo or home, Shodai parked across the street to watch from the parking lot.

Someone was running the class, and a lot of young people went in. After a while Shodai left his pickup and walked into the dojo while class was still going on. A few things struck him as being very non-traditional. First, Fred did not call the class to attention, which is standard when a black belt walks into a dojo. Shodai just said "hi Fred" and shook his hand. Neither one bowed to the other. Shodai said he thought he would drop in, then sat down to watch. Fred called over his little kids and gave them instructions. This was the beginning of his class. There were no exercises, belts on the students all askew, in Shodai's view it was a mess. He did not stay long.

The next day Fred came to see Shodai, and he bowed when he walked in, like he did the first time he came to visit. Fred said, "I just want to apologize." He was a nice guy, but something about it did not seem right. Shodai said, "when I was in your office the other day, I didn't see any certificates or anything. Who did you take from?" He said he took under Preston Carter. Shodai did not know if he was for real or not. Then Fred said he would bring his certificates to him. But Shodai said no, since he was the one that asked, he would come see him and he could show them to him. A couple days later Shodai went to see him, and he showed him a Shodan certificate. Shodai asked, "he let you have a school with only a Shodan?" He said yes because he had to leave New York. Shodai challenged him on that, saying he did not sound like he was from New York. Fred said yeah, he told Preston that he had to move for work and asked his permission to open a school. Preston Carter was a known name in the karate world. People called him stubby because he lost his legs from diabetes.

Shodai asked him if he did kata or kata kumite and Fred said, "what's kumite?" Shodai told him that some people just call it self-defense. They became pretty good friends. One day Shodai told him to bring his students over to his place and they could spar. Shodai had a small fight class one night, so he called Fred. Shodai told him that he only had a couple of students there, but he could show him what they were about. Fred brought in ten or eleven kids to Shodai's Seminary Drive dojo in Fort Worth. Shodai told his people to be easy on the visitors, almost shadow box with them. Tom Rieber and Alyce Strickland were there but Tom was low rank at the time, 3rd white. Shodai had the visiting kids sit down so they could watch his students spar first. They were trying to look bad, but they were bad actors. Pretty soon they were really getting after it. Shodai wanted to see what Fred could do, but Fred said he did not have any gear.

Shodai asked Tom to get Fred some gear from the spare box of gear and gave him a jock and cup. It was taking a long time, so Shodai went to see what was going on. Tom said Fred wouldn't come out and the gear would not fit him. Shodai went back there, and Fred apologized and said he was not prepared to fight. Shodai said "okay Fred, now I want you to take this in the best way you possibly can; you're no more a black belt than I am a green belt. I'll be your friend and you can come by and see me, but we don't have a lot in common. If you don't fight, that's what karate means, empty hands, fighting. You got to do katas, but you got to have self-defense, you should have a curriculum. You got to have some way to teach." Fred understood, and he and his students left. Shodai did not embarrass him in front of his students, but everybody knew.

Gekisai San and Choate

Jim Choate was going up for a belt test and he wanted to show his instructors a kata that was not one of their own, so he came to see Shodai. Shodai was going to sit on the panel, and Jim thought it would be good for him to do one of Shodai's katas. He asked Shodai to teach him one of his black belt katas, but unbeknownst to Choate, instead of a black belt kata, Shodai taught him Gekisai San, the third kata in the system at the time. Choate loved it. Every Tuesday and Thursday he came to the school to learn it. Sometime later Choate was at Shodai's school. Alyce Strickland was there and said, "we could count you as a black belt in our style since you learned a black belt kata." He said yeah. But then she followed with, "of course Gekisai San is only a green belt kata" followed by uncomfortable laughter.

Doctor Bob

One day a guy came into the Watauga dojo, Bob. He showed up in a Lexus and saw a picture of Ken Johnson on the wall. He told Shodai he had seen Ken Johnson at a Pat Burleson tournament and Pat gave Ken an 8th degree black belt. Then he told him that he had a black belt too, etc. and asked if he could come in and spar. Shodai stopped listening as soon as he started giving him a list of his credentials, but he asked him when the last time he worked out was. Bob said that he and some guys work out together all the time. Shodai said, "ok, you can come in tomorrow night." Bob showed up the next night with a gi slung over his shoulder, and Shodai asked him if he had any sort of tradition in his karate school? No, he said, they got away from tradition since they really did not have a school.

Bob lifted his leg straight up to the ceiling, really showing how well he could stretch. Everyone was kind of looking at him because nobody in the school really did a lot of high kicks. As is customary, Bob was paired up with a black belt, then another, and another. By the time he got to Mike Perry, Perry kicked him with a turn kick and leveled him. Shodai was watching and told him he was done. He left so fast he forgot his jacket and never came back for it.

(author's note: we looked him up on the internet after that night and it turned out he was a 5th dan in one style, 8th dan in another, etc., plus a doctor, so we referred to him as Doctor Bob after that, but he never came back.)

Motorcycle Gang

Once a guy signed up that had previously been working out at an Isshin-Ryu school. The problem was he was dirty, and it did not take long before some of the other students complained about him. Shodai told the guy to get cleaned up before he came back. The man left angrily. The next day, out of the blue, the same guy came to the dojo and wanted to fight Shodai. They went outside and the guy took a swing at him. Shodai slapped away his punch and ridge hand struck him in the jaw, then palm heeled him on the side of the face, knocking him onto the hood of his truck.

A few days later Shodai was opening the dojo, and three motorcycle riders were there ready to fight. One guy started to get off his bike and Shodai ridge hand struck him, knocking him down. A second guy turned himself around when he knocked his shoulder into a rearview mirror of a parked truck, his back to Shodai. Shodai elbowed him on the back of the head. The third guy drove off. Shodai saw the Isshin-Ryu guy, who was there too, trying to start his truck and get away. Shodai went over to him and said that if he ever saw him there again, he would whip him more than he had ever been whipped in his life. The motorcycle riders were members of a famous motorcycle gang.

Some people just want to hurt other students

There was a student in Watauga, a big guy, who signed up purely on Shodai's reputation. He had a couple of lessons but did not come back, so Shodai called him. The guy said he liked the workouts but whoever was teaching him the last night told him that when we sparred, we did not allow kicks to the leg. Shodai told him that was true. He said he had businesspeople as students, people who did not want to get their legs broken. The guy responded with, "kicks are my thing." He said he had done MMA for a while and was used to doing leg kicks. He said he could take anybody out with a leg kick. Shodai said, "you said it right there. I don't want my students coming in, paying me money, so somebody can 'take them out.'" He went on to explain that the whole idea of karate is to learn a different way of life, to protect yourself under any given situation. It did not mean when they sparred that they needed someone who liked leg kicks to 'take them out.' He told the guy he should go somewhere that has leg kicks.

Joe and Anderson

A person off the street (Joe) came to see Shodai one day and said he wanted to sign up. Shodai told him the cost and he said okay but he wanted Shodai to know that he was on probation. Apparently, he was caught robbing a house with a gun, so he did five years. He said Shodai did not have to worry about him because he had a 10 PM curfew. Once he started training, he got pretty good. He had a fast backfist, so people in the dojo started calling him LFB for Lightning Back Fist. He was skinny, but he did not drink or smoke, and eventually he got to green belt. One day Joe wrote LFB on the back of his gi. Shodai saw this and immediately told him to take it off. Shodai threw it in the trash. He said the only thing on your gi is the school patch. He was good at fighting for his rank, but his attitude was all wrong for Shodai. The next fight night Joe was paired up with Tom Rieber. Tom got him with a right hook while he was down low, a move he had made a million times. He hit everybody with it, but Joe was upset.

When it was over, Joe was nowhere to be seen. The next day Shodai was with Roy Kurban in the office and Joe came in. He asked Shodai if he wanted to know what happened to him the night before. He said yes of course, and Joe said he hid in the back; he did not want anyone to see him crying. He said he was not coming back anymore. He said there was no need for that man (Tom) to hit him as many times as he did. Joe complained that Tom never kicked; he didn't use karate. Shodai said, "did you ever fight anybody in prison?" He said yes and Shodai said "what would you do if you came up against a man like that in prison? You'd have to fight him, wouldn't you?" He said Tom hit him so many times he could not breathe. He had never been beaten like that in his life. Later he asked Tom about it, and he said he was just tapping him.

There was a man in Fort Worth who started up a Guardian Angels (the red beret wearing vigilante gang from the 1970's and 1980's) chapter named Anderson. He took two or three lessons from Shodai, then disappeared. Before he quit, Joe had come in during the day with some of his friends. He said he saw Anderson, who apparently had his own school. Joe said he went in and told him that he was doing like Musashi, going to different schools to fight. They each put on fighting gear and Joe claims to have hit him with a backfist and knocked him out with Anderson's students there to see it. He wanted Shodai to know before he was told by somebody else. Shodai told him to stay away from doing things like that. He said, "you know you're a good fighter, and I know you're good at fighting. That's enough." He mentioned that full contact was coming on, maybe he could put his fighting to good use. But he needed at least two years and a brown belt to do it.

A week later Anderson walked in and had a guy with him. Shodai played stupid and just said, "hey how's it going, haven't seen you in a while." Anderson introduced his friend, a deputy sheriff. Shodai did not give it a second thought. He was not afraid of cops. He said, "okay, what can I do for you?" The cop asked if he knew the student, Joe. He said "yeah, he's a dangerous man." Anderson said he came into his school. Shodai feigned surprise, "your school?" Shodai asked to see his certificate. Anderson said he did not walk around with it, and Shodai said he could leave right now and not come back until he brings him a certificate. He told him that you cannot just open a place and call yourself a martial artist unless you have a certificate from someone who is a real martial artist himself. This is not true of course, but Anderson turned around and left. Anderson was trying to get Shodai to incriminate himself, sending Joe over to assault him. It did not work.

Kimo Wall

Kimo Wall, former karate student of Seko Higa in Okinawa, found Shodai through one of Shodai students, Danny McDonald. Kimo came over to Shodai's dojo and stood looking at pictures on the wall. Shodai asked if he could help him. Kimo introduced himself and said he was looking for Jay Trombley. Kimo said he took a few lessons from Seikichi Toguchi as well as Seko Higa. This kind of thing always annoyed Shodai, people who took seminars from people and then called them their teacher. He said, "either you took from him two or three years or don't mention it to me." But they had a lot of history in common, each having learned Goju-Ryu in Okinawa. Finally, Kimo asked if Shodai practiced with traditional weapons and then asked if he could borrow some. He was doing a seminar and forgot his weapons. Shodai loaned him the weapons.

He came back the next day and asked Shodai if he wanted to see his nunchaku kata. Shodai politely said yes, but his kata was not the same type of weapons katas Shodai practiced. Marvin Madison, one of Shodai's black belts, came in while this was going on and went into the office giggling. He was not trying to be rude; it was just a very different kind of nunchaku kata that Marvin had never seen. When Shodai taught weapons, the weapons were intended to move with some intensity. The tournaments were not any better when it came to weapons, as live blades were forbidden on kamas, and nunchakus and bo staffs became hollow shadows of their original intention.

Tom Rieber, Ronnie Ramsey and Gillis

Tom Reiber specialized in fighting from day one. Shodai took him to Kurban's school, and he beat everybody. One night Kurban put Ronnie Ramsey with him, who was much bigger than Tom and had a lot more experience fighting. Shodai told Tom, "float like a butterfly, sting like a bee; don't let him hit you or he'll kill you." Tom got out to fight and Ronnie swung his arms so hard he would have killed him, but Tom just moved side to side. Shodai told Rieber, "fighting a guy like that, only let one foot touch the floor at the same time." Ronnie finally stopped and put his hands on his hips. A few seconds later the bell rang.

Another guy, Gillis, who had been a brown belt with Kurban for around ten years and would not test for black belt. He fought and won every tournament as a brown belt and was a great fighter. Shodai told Tom he would have to fight him. Before the fight, Tom hopped back and forth so Gillis was sure to see him. Once the bell rang, Tom went flat footed. Gillis did not know what to do. He grabbed Tom's gi to pull him in to hit him and pulled it right off his back. Tom knocked him nearly into the office with a side kick.

Norwegian Shotokan

One night three guys showed up at the Hurst dojo, two grown men black belts and a teenage brown belt. As it turned out, they were friends of one of Shodai's students, who neglected to ask Shodai if they could come in and spar. They did not bow when they came into the dojo and did not go see Shodai, which did not start things off too well with Shodai. Word got to Shodai that they were there to spar, and Shodai said okay. The dojo was full of people and there were plenty of high ranking students to spar with them. First thing, they had to get jocks and cups. They did not have any because they were not accustomed to groin strikes.

Whenever someone visited the dojo to spar, Shodai and his students were polite, but always fought visitors hard. The idea of someone coming into someone's dojo to spar was always taken as something of a challenge. It was not like the old days with Roy Kurban's school where people visited all the time. Shodai, watching the fights noticed right away that the visitors had no idea how to block groin strikes. Very loudly, Shodai told the students not to go to the groin anymore. A few minutes later Shodai noticed the visitors could not defend against ridge hand strikes either, particularly to the head. Once again, Shodai made an announcement while the sparring was going on that the students needed to stop using ridge hands. It was getting ridiculous. The visitors had great energy, particularly the younger of the two black belts, but it was clear they were not matching up at all.

(author's note: I found out later that it was not really their fault. In Shotokan, I learned, while sparring they did not fight with full contact or target the groin, and they rarely targeted the head. And this was the lesson Shodai told us after they left that night. You should never go into a school blindly and ask to spar. You need to go in first and meet the people, treat them with respect, find out their rules. That way if you do not think you can match up with them, you can stay quiet and save face. These were very polite people and were very complimentary to us after the night was over.)

Mike Stone

During the early 1980's, Steve Fisher had a tournament that Shodai and Roy Kurban attended. After the tournament they went to a restaurant, sitting in a half booth with Mike Stone. Mike Stone was a well-known martial artist who trained and then had an affair with Priscilla Presley (Elvis's wife), allegedly contributing to Elvis and Priscilla's divorce. Stone had a reputation for being wild. He was listening to the conversation at the table, but not really talking, just looking around. A few booths away four guys were doing the "shame on you" finger motion towards Stone. He got up from the table and confronted the guys, "you bunch of assholes, we'll go outside and settle this now." He went outside and the guys followed. Kurban said to Shodai that he (Stone) was the meanest guy that ever walked the earth. A few minutes later Stone came back in and sat down. His knuckles were split open, but nothing else disheveled. Shodai got up and went outside to see what happened and saw the four guys on the ground.

Luther Duffy

Luther Duffy was a Shotokan practitioner. He was known for smoking a pipe and was fluent in Japanese. He took 2nd place in kata at a Japanese tournament once, which was highly rare. Sitting at a table with George Minshew, Shodai told Duffy that he would not do well in Texas with so much hesitation in the moves, taking five minutes to do a one-minute kata. Duffy said he did not know anything else. Minshew told Duffy that he would never win if he did not change his ways, with American judges anyway.

Andrew Smith and Mark Ashraf

One day Mark Ashraf and Andrew Smith were in the dojo while Shodai sat in the office. Students were there waiting for class to start; Ashraf and Smith were punching each other in the stomach. Shodai went out and told them it was the stupidest thing he had ever seen a karate man do. Mark went into the office and asked him what he meant. Shodai said, "the whole thing." He said if you want to hit someone that badly, go into a bar and say you can whip anybody in the bar. Impatiently, Shodai told him to get his gear on. Shodai borrowed Andrew Smith's gloves and did not bother with any other equipment. Mark said, "you're going to try to knock me out." Shodai answered, "I'm not going to knock you out, but I'm going to hit you more than you hit me." The whole school was there.

Shodai got into a basic fighting stance. Mark said, "what are we going to do, kata?" Shodai just said, "no, I'm going to hit you." Mark moved around, threw a few punches and kicks, but Shodai just brushed them to the side. He knew he could not get hit by Mark because he was so strong. Mark tried to throw two punches in a row. By the time he threw the second one, Shodai saw what he wanted, got to the side and hit his arm hard, and as Mark bent over, he exposed his kidney, which Shodai immediately struck hard. At that point it was over. Shodai was doing two things: 1) showing that no matter how tough his black belts were, they should never show off how tough they are, and 2) it does not matter how big a person is, if you hit them in the kidney, the fight is going to be over quickly.

Kurban and Money

Once on a belt test at Kurban's school, Kurban, Shodai, Won Chik Park, Dennis Gotcher, and Larry Caster were on the panel. They went through half of the test, and everyone went outside for a break to talk. Gotcher oversaw the money for the test, and kept pulling money out for Kurban, who almost seemed embarrassed. Shodai told Caster that if he had a test like that, he would probably give up teaching.

Kyle Brown

Larry Caster's son broke Kyle Brown's nose while sparring at the end of a belt test. Brown weighed about 150 pounds while Caster's son was over 200. Caster's son hit him in the chest, knocked Brown back into the crowd, and as he came back up, he was knocked across the nose. Afterwards Shodai tried to set it in the office with his knuckles but could not get it to click, so Brown went to the doctor. But not before he got his belt. He would not leave until then. When he came back two weeks later, he had two black eyes.

Sanchin

A mother and father signed up their boy at the Seminary school. The boy said he did not have any friends and thought karate would be good. Soon there was a belt test that he attended, as did his mom and dad. During the test, Shodai planned on going through the Sanchin kata with strikes himself, allowing Tom Rieber to give the strikes. Before the kata, Shodai gave a speech about what Sanchin is, a test of concentration, a breathing kata at the heart of Goju-Ryu Karate. Privately Shodai told Tom to really make a show of the strikes, do it hard. Shodai started the kata and sure enough, Tom was really striking Shodai hard.

The mom and dad left, but the mom came back and tried to chastise Shodai and said, "I want to tell you something." Shodai cut her off immediately. "In here you don't tell me anything." The next day his dad came in and said thank you, and the kid came back to class.

Rusty Fralia

Rusty was Shodai's third black belt. He was in a bad motorcycle accident and had to get a trachea tube, always talked in a raspy voice after that. Shodai took over his physical therapy for him and got Rusty stronger than he'd ever been. He had him lift weights and eventually go back to doing karate. Shodai even allowed Rusty to run one of his schools for a little while.

Musical Kata

Danny McDonald and Rusty Fralia were good friends. Danny would do music kata. One day Rusty asked Shodai if he could do a musical kata. Shodai told him when he is dead and buried, and people are peeing on his grave, that is when Rusty could do a musical kata. But he really wanted to do it. Shodai relented but said he did not want it done as a Goju-Ryu kata or representing the school in any way. Rusty said he would get a gi without a school patch. Rusty did the kata and Shodai actually thought it was a pretty good kata.

(author's note: when I told Shodai that Seikichi Toguchi created a musical kata, he didn't believe me. I showed him where he talked about it in his book, and he said that disappointed him.)

The demo that didn't work

Shodai tried to explain to an audience at the school about Mushin, the state of mind of not thinking, but reacting. He wanted to talk about Sanchin and the state of mind you need to be in to do it properly. He got one of his black belts to hit him as hard as he could while he was talking. It was not to show he could take a strike, but the idea that in motion you still need to breathe. Anything you take in (breath) goes somewhere, and there must be something between taking the strikes and getting hurt. Unfortunately, the black belt threw the punch as he was turning, and the punch slid right off him. He wanted a more direct punch that landed better. He was also trying to show that he did not know where the student was punching, that in Mushin you do not have time to think. If you concentrate on what you are doing, nobody can beat you.

Alyce Strickland

Shodai had a bo staff and Alyce had a wooden sword (bokken). Alyce knocked the sword into his bo and stabbed him with the bokken, drawing blood. Karen was there and died laughing. Alyce and Shodai put the second bo kata and the bo kumite together in the 13' x 70' dojo. It took up most of the room on the floor to do it.

More on Jim Choate

Ken Taliaferro almost got into it with Jim Choate. Choate had a videotape of his rock band where he played drums. Taliaferro and Shodai were watching the tape in Choate's office. Shodai said "Damn Jim, I didn't know you had a five-piece band. What did you think of that Ken?" Taliaferro said it was okay, but the drummer was way off. Choate bowed up and got in Ken's face and said, "screw you!" Shodai said, "oh he's just kidding you."

Choate wanted a Korean title. Shodai said he'd try to find him one so he asked some Koreans what you would call someone who oversaw a company. It turned out to be "Wee Ho Ha" or something like that, so he called Choate and asked Choate if he still wanted a title. He said he had the name and told him what he found. "Screw you Trombley!"

Steve Gann was taking a black belt test under Choate, but he did not show up. Choate said, "I'll be right back", and forty-five minutes later Gann came walking through the door. Choate went over to his house and said, "you're either going to get your ass kicked by me right now or you'll get down there and take that test."

Tom's school in White Settlement

When Tom Rieber was no longer a student with Shodai, he was trying to run a school of his own on White Settlement Rd in River Oaks, but it was going broke. Shodai and Karen went over to see him at his school. Shodai offered to leave Tom his school and Tom asked if he could make it closer to his house. Shodai declined and opened a school in Hurst. Like Wado Ryu, Rieber wore a single wrap belt with the knot on the side and had his students wearing their belts over to the side. He did not use the names of the katas, referring to them as Kata 1, Kata 2, etc.

One day a man called Shodai and said he was not taking karate from Tom anymore and wanted to come back to Shodai. But Shodai refused him, saying, "no, you made your decision to quit and go with Tom." He said Shodai was too hard.

Kurban at a tournament

Steve Fisher, who was friends with Roy Kurban, threw a tournament. Shodai went to the bathroom and heard guys talking about whipping Kurban's ass; they were going to distract him and then sucker punch him. Shodai went out and told Kurban to watch out for them. Turned out one of them was slated to fight Kurban in the ring. Kurban went out and beat him easily.

From the Students

David Griffin

"I started in January of 1980. Classes were one hour long, and we worked for the entire hour, which was pretty much the same as later in time. Same routines and work over and over until karate became second nature.

The seminary school was somewhat small and worn, but we didn't care. We were there for karate, and we worked every night. Classes were Monday through Thursday with fight night on Friday. Shodai was a young Shodai at that time, so as you can imagine it was intense. One night during the moving kicking routine, I just couldn't seem to get a back heel kick all the way back. I was standing between Ken Johnson and Curtis White, with Shodai in front of me, frustrated. We must have gone up and down the floor ten times on that kick alone. I was stressed, but obviously I mastered that kick that night.

During my first four years from white belt to Shodan, we had a very tough school. I was #7 to get my name on the black belt name board. If you look at that list during that time, before and after, you know those names, and know the talent. Tournaments were special, we could hold our own against anything, and we were a traditional system. It was the real deal. Shodai was a special person who was one of the people who brought martial arts to America post WW2, military. It was life changing to anyone who spent any time there. You could apply that experience to anything in life and be confident that you are okay."

Bob Loewenstein

Interview with Bob Loewenstein by Steve Welborn (reprinted from an August 1986 Dojo Newsletter)

SW: When did you get started in UGJKA?
BL: I started in 1978, but I had a two-year layoff because I hurt my shoulder at work.

SW: Why did you get started in karate in the first place?
BL: I work at a construction company, and everybody is very big. I was smaller, so I had been taking bullying all my life and I finally got tired of it.

SW: How did you get started?

BL: I was very shy, so I waited for the school to be relatively empty. Finally, I caught Shodai at about 10:00pm with only one other person in the school. We hit it off well, so two weeks later I signed up, and I've been here ever since.

SW: Where are you from?
BL: I was born in Massachusetts, but I came down to Kansas, and then to Texas.

SW: How does it feel to be a black belt?
BL: It took me about two weeks to recover from the test, but after I got back it felt great!

SW: What is your goal?
BL: To make everything look perfect. It's hard to make some things look perfect, but you have to work hard. When you keep working, it all pays off.

SW: Do you have any advice for others?
BL: You have to make up your mind that you want to do something, and then you have to work hard and do it.

Do you have any comments about UGJKA?
BL: It's a great style. The martial arts is a full circle. Some schools teach one part of the circle, others teach another part. UGJKA teaches the whole circle. It's a complete style. They teach tradition, kata, sparring, weapons. It is a good style. If we keep having more people sign up, we can get another school, and maybe Goju will get spread all over Texas and the US, just as Tae Kwon Do has.

George Eastlick

"I appreciated that karate came first and foremost over everything else. He would only train those old enough, with thick skin, discipline, and a willingness to put in the effort required. It let you know that you were there because you were good enough, not because he needed a payday. And it spoke to the quality of instruction we all received.

I remember his grip and his forearms. He was a bear!

I enjoyed his after-class stories. But I especially enjoyed our Papa John's pizza where he relaxed a bit, and I was able to see his softer side. But whether training or relaxing, it was always about karate."

Sharon Griffin

"It was 1979, I was a kid, around ten, and David (Griffin) was thirteen. We went to dinner with my mom and my stepdad for David's 13th birthday. They gave him a gift certificate for some karate lessons at a school in our neighborhood. (Shodai's school on Seminary Dr) That's when it all began. I didn't start lessons, but I did go to tournaments and belt tests, and fight nights to watch. I got to know Ken Johnson, Shane Facemyer, Lavada White, Rusty Fralia, but I was just David's little sister. Then right after he got his black belt four years later, in 1983 I decided I wanted to try it out too!

My mom and stepdad thought after I got hit once, that I'd be done...but of course, they were wrong about that. I ended up staying and training till 1988. David and I trained every day and went to every tournament that we could. It was never on our radar that if we were tired, we didn't have to go train. If we were tired, then we just went to class and did it tired. Shodai didn't give us an option to skip class. In fact, if you weren't in class, you had better have a legitimate reason! I also ran track all through middle and high school, so most every Saturday, I was either at a track meet or a karate tournament.

Tom Reiber was there, along with Allen Crowley, Trent Boe, Mark Ashraf, and so many talented students. Ronnie Ramsey came to spar, we went to Jim Choates's school to hang out and spar, sometimes to Roy Kurban's. Everyone was all in and it was just fun and supportive. Shodai seemed very happy then and the school was booming with a lot of students, a lot of kids, and adults, and a lot of advanced ranks. There were great training partners for people of all ages. The curriculum was never boring. Shodai was intense and serious. He had no hesitation to fail you on your belt test if you made too many mistakes. He didn't want any kids under seven years old. He never wanted the dojo to be a daycare, only a serious karate school. If your gi was dirty or your belt was tied crooked, you would expect to be doing some pushups. It gave us discipline, and those that didn't like it would quit, and those of us with more dedication would stay and get better. David and I would spar in our yard. We would go fast and hard. Cars would slow down to watch us, or maybe just look at us like we were crazy. David made me tough. He would hit me hard and tell me to get mad and hit back. At tournaments he would tell me to fight those girls the way I fought him and the guys (Ken, Rusty, etc.) He said we could be friends outside the ring, but inside, I was to hit them hard and fast and not back down. I got disqualified so many times for excessive contact!

Everyone at the tournaments knew us. At a tournament one day, my stepdad beat us to the stands. A parent behind him said, "damn, the Griffin kids are here, well I guess we'll just have to settle for 2nd place today." We had so many trophies all over the house, I had over 100 and David had many too! Those tournaments were so fun. Shodai didn't always go to all of them, but he usually went to all the local ones. We would load up in the van, and travel to tournaments all over Texas. Ken Johnson would drive and sing every lyric to every song that came on the radio. At the end of the day, we would slide all the many trophies we won that day under the seats and head back to Ft Worth.

In 1988 I won 1st place in the 2nd annual Jhoon Rhee scholarship tournament. I beat his top student, who wouldn't even talk to me afterwards. They didn't want me to compete because our school wasn't a member of their Jhoon Rhee Taekwondo Association, but they took my money and let me register months prior! I had driven to Roy Kurban's school in Dallas and signed up in person! So, whoever took my money that day, I guess they didn't know. But Bob Loewenstein went to bat for me that day (Shodai had been there all day at the regular tournament but had gotten a bad headache and went home so he didn't see me compete.) After Bob talked to them, they decided to let me compete. They never thought I would win. I don't remember who our judges were that day. One was Grand Master Jose Santamaria, and the others may have been Roy Kurban, or some other "elders", but they were always our judges at all the AOK tournaments, so I don't remember exactly who we had that evening. I was also the only female competitor. There were 5 students competing at that day from different schools. I sparred the guys and did kata (the only one to do kata without music, just the traditional way.) I was mad and fought those guys the way David had taught me to fight! I won in sparring and beat them in kata with Juhito! When they called my name as the winner you could have heard a pin drop. Then someone started clapping, and then everyone started cheering! It was a great moment, but Shodai missed that. My mom was there, and Bob Loewenstein was there. There was no ceremony, recognition, nothing! Jhoon Rhee just said he'd send me a check in the mail. The first Jhoon Rhee scholarship tournament a year prior had 2 female competitors and was held in Cleburne, and there was a presentation of a trophy and the scholarship check to the two ladies who had competed. For me, that day, nothing! And like he said, a couple weeks later I got a check from Jhoon Rhee's personal bank account in the mail for $3000 (in 1987), no congratulations letter or recognition. That's the day I lost all respect for the Grandmaster of Taekwondo, so it was bittersweet, and it did feel good to beat his top student and to cash that check! God's honest truth, that was one of my best wins and Shodai missed it, which I have always been a little bitter about. But he threw me a surprise party afterwards at the Hurst school. Everyone came and that was fun.

Shodai was a serious teacher, all business, but I was never scared of him, or reluctant of being yelled at. If he yelled at me, I knew it was because I forgot something, or he was just pushing me to do better. He rarely yelled at me though. Really, I only remember him just pushing me: hit harder, kick harder, do it again. I was a quick learning student, and he was proud. I knew he was proud of all of us at that time during those high school years. The school had a big black and white sign out front, and big windows, with a few chairs for spectators. Spectators were always welcome. Folks would just come in off the street to see what we were doing. Sometimes on Wednesday night fight nights we would have 2 rings going and a full school with yelling and cheering and impressive sparring. I remember people walking by couldn't help but stop in and watch. There was a raised wood floor, lots of blisters till your feet got tough, always using the metal mallet to hammer down the nails that loosened up, bamboo walls, mirrors, the Japanese flag, and pictures of his lineage, just simple, old, and traditional, dank and smelled like a combination of sweat and musty old fighting gear. I loved that place, so many hours we spent there, and so many memories, great fight nights, so many people would show up, lots and lots of sparring, a lot of fun!

I was a freshman in college at U.T. Arlington, my parents had moved to the country, and David was a firefighter at age 19. He had moved out and bought his first house in Fort Worth. I moved in with him to be closer to school, but I didn't have money. I went to bartending school at age 18 and wanted to focus on my college classes and had to work to pay for it. I was working nights. I told Shodai I was leaving to be a bartender. He wasn't too happy about that, but it is what it is. He always welcomed me back. I transferred to UT Austin shortly after that and moved. I still was welcomed back anytime I was home visiting. But my adult life was built in Austin, so I didn't make it back too often. I think after a few years, I was invited to sit on the panel at Ashley (Oliver's) black belt test. That was so fun to get to go back for that!

As for karate and me, in the past thirty years I've spent in Austin, I have trained in over a dozen dojos! In the beginning when I was a black belt, I knew many instructors down here. Roy Kurban's student, Dennis Gotcher had a school. Bobby Santamaria (Jose's little brother had a school), also Stanley Hill, Michael Abideen are a few names of instructors that knew me from the AOK tournaments over the years. But I was in college, working 2 jobs, so I never stuck around those schools, just went every now and then to work out or spar with them. I was even invited to a special Friday night "fight night" invitation only to black belts of different schools and styles who wanted to meet after hours at a dojo. I was the only female in that group. Those guys taught me how to box, and my sparring improved a lot. I've gotten a brown belt, (Shito Ryu), Orange belt (Shotokan - did that at the gym for a year with my daughter Jessi, when she was 7), Blue belt (2 years of Bakido - lots of flips and takedowns, kind of hard for me at age 44), another year learning Soryu with Rudy Vasquez but that was because I was doing fitness kickboxing with him. A whole lot of kickboxing, no gi's or karate, just plain old working out with focus pads, bags & ring sparring. I taught step aerobics for years and taught kickbox aerobics too, and that was so fun!

In my later years, it was always for fitness. I never stayed at one dojo because they were never the same. I had so many reasons to leave, many pros and cons, one school was at the gym, they didn't have their own dedicated dojo so we would be in the aerobics room, and folks would just come in and try to stretch or whatever and we'd run them out of there, so there was no dedicated place for us. I hated that! Or a school was great, and I would like the instructor, but they had no adults, or advanced adults for me to train with so I'd be bored, or the curriculum would just suck, katas were boring, and they were sloppy and would fly through all different speeds, no discipline, or consistency and I hated that! Or maybe they had a great curriculum, and lots of advanced adults to train with but they didn't spar, ever. (Bakido) Or a great school with a good curriculum, but they would hold me back. I'm no white belt, but if you treated me like one, I was not staying. If after class I go to the side and do hook kicks better than anyone in the room, yet during class since I'm new, and in their curriculum it's a green belt skill and I'm told to stand to the side. I'm not staying around where I'm patronized and held back or treated like a beginner. But I will say that only happened once, and after the instructor saw my kicks "outside of class time", I was soon leading the whole class in an advanced kick routine. But in other schools, with not learning anything new, not feeling challenged, not given an opportunity to reach my potential or just being always paired with other beginners when I'm not a beginner, I was not staying around. Sure, I was older and didn't look like I was a black belt, but all I needed was a chance to dust off the cobwebs and get going again. And when I was in schools that had sparring and every time they said "we won't promote you too many levels at once, you'll have to move up through all the ranks like everyone else, but after a few months "well we are gonna make an exception for you, cause you obviously don't spar like a beginner and it's misleading, we are gonna test you up to brown belt, etc., but I was bored, so VERY bored!

Shodai ruined every school for me that I would ever try to make a new home! No sparring? Sloppy katas? Arrogant instructors that taught sloppy karate? I would ultimately leave. Fast Forward a few years, I was excited to try another Goju-Ryu school here in Austin. It was a very traditional school with very traditional curriculum. They had some great students. I stuck it out for 6 months, but after Shodai's curriculum, I honestly never felt challenged or felt I had the opportunity to practice to my full potential. After 6 months we had only done very basic kicks and strikes, the pace was going to be too slow for me. I was frequently placed with beginners and just found myself bored and discontented. A few more years passed and my old friend who is a black belt in Shotokan (where we trained together at the gym) called me up and said to get the dust and cobwebs off your gi, we're gonna go train again at this new school that just opened less than 10 minutes from your house! She was our instructor at Shotokan at the gym and my training partner. She had left and after that I had no advanced partners and had really missed her. This time I was totally humbled, and enough time had passed that I had really emptied my cup, and could learn a different style, but injuries have kept me away.

My 22 years on the fire engine wrecked my back, and I've spent thousands of dollars on orthopedic problems for my feet. I once hated all the schools because they didn't have wooden floors like they were supposed to! I hated mats, and carpet, you're not supposed to do karate on mats or carpets, but now I can't do anything barefoot, so mats are good for an older person doing karate! I also tore my shoulder a few years back, couldn't punch, then 4 years ago I broke my hand and had 2 surgeries to try and fix it, but it healed wrong, and I still can't make a proper fist, plus it's painful to hit anything because of the scar tissue that limits the range of motion in my hand. And now that my body can't do karate in a way that matches what my brain thinks it's supposed to feel like, it's just less fun. Karate was always fun, but it was most fun with

Shodai in those early years!

Anyway, that's my personal history with karate, about how I have loved it my whole life and how training in Shodai's school all those years ago on Seminary Dr would have huge impact on my life for decades to follow. It also made every other school pale in comparison. I have never found one that made me feel like home. I know Shodai went to Japan and trained for a few short years, then came back and just declared himself a 10th degree black belt without testing for it under anyone. He made up his own style. But what he did was genius. He added the right amount of curriculum, with challenging katas, and routines, kumites, kata kumites, self-defense, weapons, wazas, bagwork, sparring. It is a very well rounded, balanced, effective, and challenging curriculum. Not too easy and not too hard. It challenged and pushed you yet gave you self-efficacy and confidence as you worked your way up the ranks. It had hard and soft style techniques, many different stances, and angles, open hand strikes, elbows, knee strikes, etc. It was never boring. He may have had a lot of personality conflicts with folks over the years, but when it came to karate and training, he was the most passionate instructor. He pulled the best out of you, and he expected nothing less. I trained with Shodai for about 5 years, and then I went on to train with other schools for more years than I spent with Shodai. I honestly lost count. I learned so much more, and enjoyed the other styles, but the more I trained in other schools under other instructors, the more I realized that Shodai's karate was the best. But seriously of all the excuses and reasons I left the other schools, the one recurring reason is that I was just bored! If I had not left Ft. Worth, I would have stayed for many more years.

Those 5 years in the early 80's doing karate were some of the very best years of my life! So Shodai single handedly made me love karate for 5 years, then hate it every single time I tried to go back. Shodai was the foundation that cultivated my love for the sport, the best karate ever, yet was the beginning of my discontent in every school after, as the shoes were just too big to fill."

Robert Oliver

"I met Shodai in 2002. My wife Ashley was a returning student after we moved to the mid-cities (between Dallas and Fort Worth). I had been up to the dojo once or twice, and finally met Shodai after a belt test. I came to see Ashley re-test for 3rd kyu brown belt, which wasn't too unusual for a returning student. He didn't introduce himself as Shodai, but as Jay. In fact, he said people called him Crazy Jay. He was shorter than I thought he would be, but stout. He looked like one of those older guys you figured had maybe been through a few things and knew how to handle himself. He was casual, but you knew he was in charge. I was interested in joining after what I saw on the belt test, and Shodai seemed friendly enough. He was not a Mr. Miyagi type by any means. He was boisterous and did not seem to have any fear of repercussions at all. You could tell by the way he talked that he didn't care if he burned bridges or made a best friend – he was going to be honest with those around him, making sure his circle of friends was very small, despite knowing some of the most influential people in karate for decades.

Over time I learned that he called people out on their bull (whether he was right or not) and cut people out of his life at the drop of a hat if he thought they slighted him. But despite this guarded nature, there was something about him, and I completely trusted his karate. His advanced students were phenomenal, and you just knew he could turn anyone into a great fighter. I got to know him better over the years and realized his failings were built out of insecurities, like most people. But he never really changed from the moment I met him. No matter what his health was, he was the same, and there's something comforting about a person like that. But at the same time, I knew why some people couldn't get along with him.

When Shodai first saw me, he was less than pleased. The way he remembers it, "We were having class and I saw you with all these tattoos. I said who in the hell is this? I hard-started for you and Loewenstein stopped me and said no, that's Ashley's husband. I thought you were in a motorcycle gang. As soon as you left, Ashley came into the office and told him who you were."

Shodai didn't instruct me too much at first, leaving that to Chris Collins, the black belt who practically ran the school at the time. But after Chris left, Shodai taught the intermediate and advanced classes. In the intermediate class he made us take turns calling out the routines and would be visibly annoyed if we didn't know what the next kick, punch, or block was. I tried to pay close attention to the way he taught students, the little details about the katas, or the reasons he put certain things in the system, etc. because starting around green belt I wanted my own school. I also figured out that if Shodai told you something, or said something in front of you, he expected you to recall it on demand. This would prove to be challenging because there was always so much to take in, but luckily, he repeated a lot of the same stories.

Shodai had incredible attention to detail. He never let anyone get away with sloppy form. Once we were doing Gekisai San kata as a group. The end is tricky when you first learn it, mainly the hand and foot combination. We had to do it over and over, each person by themselves in front of the group while he critiqued it, "no, no, like this!" Years later, after he retired, I asked him about the ending of that kata, and he got me out on the dojo floor at my school. He said, "nobody ever does the ending right, but it's like this," and then he showed me. It was close to how I had been practicing and teaching it, but not exactly. I had to re-teach the ending of the kata, which was maddening, but necessary. Another moment that stands out was when I was learning Kumite Rokyu (a two-man exercise) with Ken Taliaferro. Shodai sat on the railing behind us and every time I hesitated or did the counter wrong, he made us stop and go back to the first one, starting all over again. It was long, tedious, and I'm sure Ken was getting annoyed, as he tried to whisper moves to me if I started to pause. It was frustrating to me too, but I knew there was no choice. I had to remember the moves. Do it again, again, again, again, again.

As an advanced rank, especially at black belt, I was glad not to be the highest rank because the highest rank always got the most pressure from Shodai. I felt bad for Ken Taliaferro because Shodai was on his case constantly. He simply was not allowed to forget anything. He was hard on all his black belts, but he was especially hard with Taliaferro. But the maddest I ever saw Shodai get at me was on a fight night when I was the only black belt there. We had a visitor from Ken's Springtown dojo, a green belt, but I forgot about him once class started. That night we also had visitors who wanted to watch a class. This green belt had the exact same body shape and fighting style as one of our then brown belts, George Eastlick. At brown belt we allow face contact and, being blind as a bat without my glasses, during the fight I punched the guy right between the eyes. I knew what I had done as soon as it happened, so I stopped to check on him, hoping it was just a little pop. But no, blood started to pour from his forehead where it cut him open. His face was not conditioned yet and he bled easily. I knew it was my fault. Shodai came over and popped me in the chest with his back to the spectators so they couldn't see him. It took him a few days before he would even speak to me.

Time passed and Shodai retired in 2016. As the only acknowledged student with a school, I was promoted to 9th Dan, the successor to Shodai, and was made President of KGJKA (Ketsugo Goju-

Ryu Karate Association). That honor could have gone to many other people who made Black Belt under Shodai before me, and many of them vastly more talented. The first obvious choice to me was David Griffin, Shodai's first 3rd Dan and hands down the best student Shodai ever had. David, unfortunately, wasn't running his own school and it didn't look like it was going to happen any time soon. David and I trained together as black belts and was an incredible training partner. He wasn't just great at karate; he could teach it better than anyone except Shodai. At one time the successor might have been Chris Collins. When I joined, Chris ran all the classes and despite his young age, could do it all. Unfortunately, Chris left Shodai to learn MMA. But Chris was always complimentary of Shodai and his karate system. It didn't take long before Chris made up with Shodai, and even started his own MMA school in Shodai's old Hurst location when we were all in Watauga. Unfortunately, Chris had a bad heart and died in 2012 at the age of 34. When Chris left the school, Bob Loewenstein soon followed. He had been Shodai's friend for a long time, and without going into any details, Shodai asked him to leave the school. This was about 2003, and by this point the lead student was Ken Taliaferro. He had his own dojo in Springtown, and after everything he had gone through with Shodai, one day in the Spring of 2009 his gear was gone from the black belt dressing room. We never saw him again. A month or so later he spoke to Shodai on the phone, and everything seemed okay, but he never came back. Ken spent nearly every night at the dojo at the expense of his own family and dojo and was a wonderful teacher. I will never forget how well he prepared me for my first black belt test as he was going for his 5th degree black belt. As a 2nd degree black belt, he knocked me out cold when his shin connected with the corner of my forehead! Still, it was great training with him, Mike Perry, Brodie Wolgamott, and my wife Ashley as I climbed the ranks.

In 2012 I opened my own dojo in Bedford, Texas. A few months later Shodai promoted me to 5th and Griffin to 6th. But eventually Griffin stopped coming in altogether, being busy with life as a fire fighter, ambulance worker, and his house was all the way out in Cleburne. By 2016, Shodai's school only had about four or five students and he'd had enough. He shut it down on a Thursday, and I inherited 3 new students from Shodai, including Shodai's last black belt Cliff Knudson. That fall, October 6th he promoted me to 9th Dan and officially signed his system over to me. It was a proud moment, to be sure, but a strange one too. I didn't feel like I deserved the promotion at all. People that high of rank are in their 70's or 80's and had been doing karate for 60 years. I was a fourteen-year student and only forty-five years old at the time. It is true, I never stopped training with Shodai since I started, but it was more situational than anything else as the reason I took over the system. I often wonder how it felt for Seikichi Toguchi, Eiichi Miyazato, and Meitoku Yagi to promote themselves to black belt in 1953 just so they could promote Goju-Ryu Karate. They had to promote themselves because their instructor, the creator of Goju-Ryu Karate didn't name a successor. Shodai didn't make the same mistake. He always said that his successor would be the highest ranked black belt at the time of his choosing. He chose me and I take the responsibility seriously. I promised Shodai that I would keep his system going as long as I lived and would keep it strong.

After retirement Shodai came to see me at my school every couple of weeks, always on a Saturday at 10am. When he came, I had coffee with him and Karen and he would tell me stories, many that I'd heard 100 times. When the pandemic hit in 2020, I could only talk to him on the phone. Then after a while I was able to go see him, so I visited him at his house on a regular basis, but in retrospect not nearly as often as I wish I did. Seeing Shodai's health deteriorate before my eyes, I purposely asked him specific questions I could write down afterwards. His memories were too important to die out, and most of what I put in this book came from those talks."

Appendix

Founders and their Styles

Founder	Style
Jigoro Kano (1860-1938)	**Judo** (studied Jujutsu)
Gichin Funkakoshi (1868-1957)	**Shotokan** (studied Shuri Te)
Choki Motobu (1870-1944)	**Motobu-Ryu** (studied Shuri Te, Tomari Te)
Kanbun Uechi (1877-1948)	**Uechi-Ryu** (studied Pangai -noon)
Morihei Ueshiba (1883-1969)	**Aikido** (studied Daito-Ryu Aiki-Jujutsu)
Chibana Choshin (1885-1969)	**Shorin-Ryu** (studied Shuri Te)
Kyoda Juhatsu (1887-1968)	**To-on-Ryu** (studied Naha Te)
Chojun Miyagi (1888-1953)	**Goju-Ryu** (studied Naha Te, Pa Kua Chang, Shaolin Chuan)
Hohan Soken (1889-1982)	**Matsumura Seito Shorin-Ryu** (studied Shorin-Ryu)
Kenwa Mabuni (1889-1952)	**Shito-Ryu** (studied Shuri Te, Naha Te)
Hironori Otsuka (1892-1982)	**Wado-Ryu** (studied Jujutsu, Shotokan)
Shoshin Nagamine (1907-1997)	**Matsubayashi-Ryu** (studied Shuri Te)
Tatsuo Shimabuku (1908-1975)	**Isshin-Ryu** (studied Shorin-Ryu, Goju-Ryu)
Gogen Yamaguchi (1909-1989)	**Goju-Kai** (studied Goju-Ryu)
Meitoku Yagi (1912-2003)	**Meibukan Goju-Ryu** (studied Goju-Ryu)
Seikichi Toguchi (1917-1998)	**Shoreikan Goju-Ryu** (studied Goju-Ryu)
Eiichi Miyazato (1922-1999)	**Jundokan Goju-Ryu** (studied Goju-Ryu)
Masutatsu Oyama (1923-1994)	**Kyokushin-Kai** (studied Shotokan, Goju-Ryu)
Ed Parker (1931-1990)	**American Kempo** (studied Kenpo Jujitsu)
Peter Urban (1934-2004)	**USA Goju** (studied Goju-Kai, Butokukai)
Jay Trombley (1938-2022)	**Ketsugo Goju-Ryu** (studied Shoreikan Goju-Ryu, Kobudo, American Boxing, Jujitsu)
Bruce Lee (1940-1973)	**Jeet Kune Do** (studied Wing Chun Kung Fu, Tai Chi, Boxing)
Chuck Norris (1940-)	**American Tang Soo Do** (studied Tang Soo Do)

Martial Arts Timeline

6th Century: Bodhidharma taught the Shaolin Monks (estimated date)

1609 - Shimazu Tadatsune, Lord of Satsuma, invaded the Ryukyu Kingdom resulting in the kings of the Ryukyus paying tribute to the Japanese shogun as well as to the Chinese emperor, further enforcement of weapons bans for the Ryukyus

1670 – Kusanku born

1683 – Peichin Takahara born

1733 – Kangi Sakugawa born

1750 – Kangi Sakugawa began training under Peichin Takahara

1756 – Kangi Sakugawa began training Chuan Fa under Kusanku

1760 – Peichin Takahara died

1762 – Kusanka died

1786 – Kanga Sakugawa born

1809 – Sokon "Bushi" Matsumura born

1815 – Kangi Sakugawa died

1831 – Anko Itosu born

1840 – Seisho Arakaki born

1853 - Kanryo Higashionna born, March 10th

1867 - Kanryo Higashionna began studying Leohan Quan from Seisho Arakaki & Kojo Taite; Kanga Sakugawa died

1868 – Gichin Funakoshi born, Nov 10th

1870 - Higashionna traveled to Fuzhou China to study Chinese Kempo (Pan Gainoon) from Wai Xinxian, Kojo Tatai, and principally Ryu Ryu Ko; Choki Motobu born, April 5th; Chotoku Kyan born

1874 – Ryukyu Islands terminated tribute relations with China

1879 - Ryukyu Islands annexed to Japan as the Okinawa Prefecture

1881 - Higashionna returned to Naha, Okinawa where his martial arts would be known as Naha-Te

1886 – Chotoku Kyan began studying under Sokon Matsumura

1888 - Chojun Miyagi born, April 25th

1889 – Hohan Soken born, May 25th

1890 – Chotoku Kyan began studying Tomari-Te with Kosaku Matsumora and Kokan Oyadomari

1898 – Seiko Higa born, Nov 8th

1899 – Miyagi began studying with Ryuko Arakaki; Sokon "Bushi" Matsumura died

1901 – Jin'an Shinzato born, Feb 5th

1902 - Miyagi began studying Naha-Te with Kanryo Higashionna

1908 – Anko Itosu wrote *Ten Precepts of Karate*; Tatsuo Shimabuku born, Sept 19th

1909 – Gogen Yamaguchi born, Jan 20th

1911 – Seiko Higa began training under Kanryo Higashionna

1912 – Meitoku Yagi born, March 6th

1915 - Miyagi traveled to Fujian Province to learn Chinese Kempo as Higashionna had done; Kanryo Higashionna died in October; Anko Itosu died, March 11th

1917 – Seikichi Toguchi born, May 20th

1918 – Seisho Arakaki died

1921 – Tensho kata is formalized by Chojun Miyagi

1922 – Ei'ichi Miyazato born, July 5th; Gichin Funakoshi introduced karate to mainland Japan; Tatsuo Shimabuku began studying Shorin-Ryu karate under Chotoku Kyan

1923 – Masutatsu (Mas) Oyama born July 27th; Robert Trias born, Mar 18th

1928 – Jackie Simpson, Florida boxer had his debut fight on Sept 28th against Clever Moro which ended in a draw

1930 – The All-Japan Martial Arts Demonstration was held in Kyoto. Miyagi's top student Jin'an Shinzato went and when asked about his style was unable to answer. This was the impetus that encouraged Chojun Miyagi to name his style. He chose Goju-Ryu after a line in the Bubishi.

1931 – Seiko Higa opened a dojo in Kumoji, Naha; Ed Parker born, Mar 19th

1932 – Chojun Miyagi's version of Sanchin is formalized; Jhoon Rhee born, Jan 7th

1933 - Goju-ryu was officially recognized as a budo in Japan by Dai Nippon Butoku Kai, recognized as a modern martial art, or gendai budo by the Japanese Government

1934 – Miyagi wrote Karate-do Gaisetsu; received title of Kyoshi from Dai Nippon Butokukai

1935 – Jackie Simpson ended his boxing career in a KO win against Mike Gonzalez, July 30th

1936 - Miyagi trained with Miao Xing in Monk Fist Kung Fu in Shanghai; Gichin Funakoshi built the first Shotokan dojo in Tokyo; J Pat Burleson born April 27th

1938 – Harvey Leighton (Jay) Trombley born, Nov 2nd; Don Nagle born; Jigoro Kano died

1940 – Miyagi created the katas Gekisai Dai Ichi & Gekisai Dai Ni; Allen Steen born; Chuck Norris born March 10th; Bruce (Jun-Fan) Lee born Nov 27th; Seiko Higa received Renshi title from Dai Nippon Butokukai

1944 – Choki Motobu died, April 15th; Joe Lewis born, March 7th

1945 - American military control over Okinawa began; Chotoku Kyan died, Sept 20th; Jhoon Rhee began training in martial arts under Nam Tae Hi; Bill Wallace born, Dec 1st; Jin'an Shinzato died, Mar 31st

1946 – Skipper Mullins born, April 25th; Dai Nippon Butokukai dissolved by occupying American force; Mas Oyama began training in Shotokan Karate; Robert Trias opened first Caucasian run dojo in the United States in Phoenix Arizona

1947 – Mas Oyama began training in Goju-Ryu Karate with Nei-Chu So (student of Chojun Miyagi)

1948 – Gogen Yamaguchi opened his dojo; United States Karate Association (USKA) formed by Robert Trias, the first karate organization on the American mainland

1949 – Gichin Funakoshi's students created the Japan Karate Association (JKA)

1950 – Gogen Yamaguchi established All Japan Karate-do Goju-kai; Demetrius "Greek" Havanas born

1952 - Miyagi's senior students created an organization to promote the growth of Goju-ryu called Goju-ryu Shinkokai ("Association to Promote Goju-ryu"), the founding members were Seko Higa, Keiyo Matanbashi, Jinsei Kamiya, and Genkai Nakaima; The Ryukyu Provisional Central Government became the Government of the Ryukyu Islands

1953 - Chojun Miyagi died, Oct 8th; Miyagi's senior students promoted themselves to black belt; Meitoku Yagi opened his Meibukan Goju-Ryu dojo in Daido, Naha, Okinawa; Bruce Lee began studying Wing Chun under Ip Man; Mas Oyama opened up Oyama Dojo in Tokyo

1954 – Miyagi's advanced students voted unanimously to name Ei'ichi Miyazato as the successor of Chojun Miyagi; Seikichi Toguchi opened the Shoreikan Goju-Ryu dojo in Koza City, Okinawa; Ed Parker founded American Kempo Karate and opened a dojo in Provo, Utah

1955 - Jay Trombley enlisted in the US Marine Corps, joined Shoreikan Goju-Ryu dojo with Seikichi Toguchi, Oct 19th, soon after began learning kobudo from Hohan Soken

1956 – Ei'ichi Miyazato opened his Jundokan Goju-Ryu dojo in Asato, Naha, Okinawa; Tatsuo Shimabuku renamed his Chan Mi Te style Isshin-Ryu; Ed Parker opened a dojo in Pasadena, California

1957 – Gichin Funakoshi died, April 26th; May Oyama founded Kyokushinkai Karate-Do

1958 – Chuck Norris began training in Tang Soo Do while in the US Air Force stationed in Korea

1960 - Jay Trombley left Okinawa with a black belt and a teaching certificate from Seikichi Toguchi

1961 – Trombley began teaching karate in Florida at Johnny Joca's gym and began learning boxing from Jackie Simpson

1962 – Chuck Norris opened a martial arts studio in Torrance, California

1963 – Allen Steen and J Pat Burleson received black belts under Jhoon Rhee; Skipper Mullins began training in Tae Kwon Do in October under Allen Steen

1964 – Bruce Lee performed his famous self-defense demonstration at the Long Beach International Karate Championships in California

1965 - Roy Kurban began studying Tae Kwon Do under Allen Steen, Larry Caster, and Skipper Mullins

1966 – Seko Higa died Apr 16th

1968 - Joe Lewis won the first professional karate tournament in both Kansas City, Missouri and Dallas, Texas

1970 – Roy Kurban, stationed in Korea with US Army, trained in Tae Kwon Do under Won Chik Park

1971 - Jay Trombley moved to Texas, taught karate out of his home in Springtown Texas

1972 - Okinawan administrative rights reverted to Japan

1973 – Trombley married Karen Kitto, Feb 17th; Bruce Lee died, July 20th

1974 – Trombley formed United Goju-Ryu Karate Association; Greek Havanas, full contact fighter out of Dallas won the grand championship at the US Karate Association Grand Nationals; Professional Karate Association (PKA) formed to promote the sport of full contact karate

1975 - Tatsuo Shimabuku died, May 30th; Greek Havanas won the PKA US Welterweight Championship

1981 – Demetrius "Greek" Havanas died in a plane crash, July 23rd (pallbearers included Skipper Mullins, Jack Hwang and Chuck Norris)

1982 – Hohan Soken died, Nov 30th; KICK (Karate International Council of Kickboxing) organized by Frank Babcock, Larry Caster, Roy Kurban, Bob Wall, and Fred Wren (Chuck Norris was the goodwill ambassador)

1984 - Trombley took the title "Shodai" meaning founder and assigned himself 10th Dan after 10 years of running his own martial arts system and 29 years in the martial arts

1989 – Gogen Yamaguchi died, May 20th; Robert Trias died, July 11th

1990 – Ed Parker died, Dec 15th

1994 – Mas Oyama died, Apr 26th

1998 - Dai Nippon Butokukai recognized Goju-ryu Karate-do as an ancient form of martial art (koryu) and as a bujutsu; Seikichi Toguchi died, Aug 31st

1999 – Ei'ichi Miyazato died, Dec 11th; Don Nagle died, Aug 23rd

2003 – Meitoku Yagi died, Feb 7th

2005 - Shodai changed the name of his organization to the Ketsugo Goju-Ryu Karate Association (KGJKA)

2012 – Joe Lewis died, Aug 31st

2016 – Shodai retired from karate after 61 years in the martial arts, named R. Oliver as his successor

2018 - Jhoon Rhee died, Apr 30th

2020 – Skipper Mullins died, May 15th

2021 – Oliver Karate Academy (KGJKA) closed in Bedford Texas, June 1st; Bryant Karate Academy (KGJKA) opened in North Richland Hills Texas, June 1st; J Pat Burleson died, Oct 31st

2022 – Oliver Karate Academy (KGJKA) re-opened in Colorado Springs, March; Shodai Jay Trombley died, Nov 23rd

KGJKA Senior Black Belt Shodan Dates

1978 – (1) Alyce Strickland (8/25)
1980 – (2) Tom Rieber (2/9)
1981 – (3) Rusty Fralia (6/7)
       (4) Todd Kauffman (6/7)
1983 – (5) Lavada White (10/9)
       (6) Shane Facemyer (10/9)
1984 – (7) David Griffin (4/15)
       (8) Ken Johnson
1986 – (9) Bob Loewenstein (5/31)
       (10) Mark Ashraf (11/8)
1987 – (11) Sharon Griffin (9/26)
       (12) Allen Crowley (9/26)
1989 – (13) Marshall Van Norden (2/18)
1990 – (14) Christine Landmon (6/23)
1992 – (15) Kyle Brown (2/29)
       (16) Andrew Smith (2/29)
       (17) Marvin Madison (2/29)
       (18) Russell Dare (7/10)
1995 – (19) Chris Collins (9/15)
1998 – (20) Kenneth Taliaferro
       (21) Jared Smith
2001 – (22) Alan Viengluang (6/14)
2002 – (23) Trent Boe (10/24)
       (24) Mike Perry (10/24)
       (25) Brodie Wolgamott (10/24)
2005 – (26) Ashley Oliver (5/13)
2007 – (27) Robert Oliver (6/22)
2010 – (28) George Eastlick (10/28)
2012 – (29) Cliff Knudson (9/27)
2018 – (30) Tim Bryant (11/17)
       (31) Armando Navarro (11/17)

Ketsugo Goju-Ryu Schools

Honbu Dojo (Home School)
Oliver Karate Academy
Colorado Springs, Colorado
(719) 581-3161
www.oliverkarate.com

Branch Dojo
Bryant Karate Academy
North Richland Hills, Texas
(682) 325-9755
www.bryantkarateacademy.com